PR RAINMAKER

PR Rainmaker

Three Simple Rules
for Using the News Media
to Attract Customers and Clients

Rusty Cawley

Writers Club Press

San Jose New York Lincoln Shanghai

PR Rainmaker
Three Simple Rules
for Using the News Media
to Attract Customers and Clients

Writers Club Press
an imprint of iUniverse, Inc.

For information address:
iUniverse, Inc.
5220 S. 16th St., Suite 200
Lincoln, NE 68512
www.iuniverse.com

ISBN: 0-595-24399-1

Printed in the United States of America

Contents

Introduction:
Learning to Think
Like a PR Rainmaker

I.a Who should become a PR Rainmaker?

The answer is: Anyone who wants to generate high-impact publicity that will attract clients, customers and revenue.

PR Rainmaking is more than a package of ready-made tactics. It is a strategic approach to thinking about the news media and how they can be used to:

- Gain attention.

- Establish credibility.

- Enhance reputation.

- Advance causes.

- Confront issues.

- Attract prospects.

- Add customers.

Entrepreneurs can use PR Rainmaking to make their ideas credible to lenders and investors. Once a company is launched, the entrepreneur can then use PR Rainmaking to open doors for the sales force and to lay the groundwork for going public.

Business executives can use PR Rainmaking to improve the reputation of a mature company or to establish the credibility of a young enterprise. Companies that are viewed as winners have a much easier time attracting customers and employees, according to one 1999 study by Yankelovich Partners. The study also showed that "winners" tend to do better on Wall Street, enjoying higher multiples on their stock prices, and thus significantly larger market caps.

Professionals can use PR Rainmaking to establish themselves in the public mind as top experts in their fields. Potential clients often turn first to the names they see appear consistently in the news media.

Not-for-profit executives can use PR Rainmaking to advance their causes, to put their issues on the public agenda and to improve fund-raising results. Donors tend to give generously to the causes that appear to be in the most immediate need of attention, and tend to make their judgments based on what they see in the news media.

Anyone can use PR Rainmaking to advance a career, launch an enterprise, create a brand name, raise capital, attract a crowd, identify a worthy cause, spur action from the public or even fight City Hall.

Who can become a PR Rainmaker? You can.

Who should become a PR Rainmaker? You should.

I.b The PR Rainmaker's Motto

PR Rainmaking is to marketing what sweat equity is to real estate. You can't buy it. You've got to work for it, and work hard.

The PR Rainmaker embraces this motto: "There's no such thing as 'free' publicity."

So why make the effort?

There are three reasons.

First, PR Rainmaking will establish your credibility. It will position you in the public mind as an expert in your field. How? The media will quote you, write about you, follow your progress and lend you a third-party endorsement that cannot be purchased with advertising.

Second, PR Rainmaking will raise your visibility. It will put you in the public eye. When handled properly, it will transform you into a well-regarded brand.

Third, PR Rainmaking will make your phone ring with higher quality clients and customers.

Make no mistake: It takes time, effort and persistence to become a PR Rainmaker. But the rewards are well worth the price you pay.

I.c The Secret to Understanding the News Media

The first step to becoming a PR Rainmaker is to learn to think like a PR Rainmaker. You must reject much of what you have learned about PR and much of what others think about PR.

Using PR as a rainmaking tool requires a separate set of fundamentals than other forms of PR, such as corporate communications, community relations or issues management.

PR Rainmaking is specifically about using publicity to attract prospects who are likely to become clients or customers. To reach these prospects, you must gain the willing cooperation of the news media: print, broadcast or Web.

You must understand fundamentally what most of your peers fail to grasp: The news is just one more consumer product, just as certainly as cola, soap and toilet tissue. The news media are manufacturers and distributors of that news.

And that makes you, the PR Rainmaker, a supplier of raw materials for the news media.

I.d Why News is Like Fish

The news media have done an amazing job of positioning themselves in the public mind.

Almost no one speaks of the "news business."

Instead, Americans tend to think of the news media as more like government and religion than like fast-food chains and supermarkets. We see the media as institutions designed to serve us, not as enterprises designed to separate us from our cash.

The media accomplished this feat by persistently referring to themselves as "The Fourth Estate." Journalists will tell you that they "crusade for the First Amendment" and "fight for the public's right to know."

It's all very heartwarming.

It's also bunk.

The Founders understood the true role of the news media even as they penned the Bill of Rights in 1789. (They met in secret, by the way; so much for the public's "right to know.") To them, the press had two purposes. One was as a means of political persuasion. The other was as a pure business enterprise.

That's why—in the days of Washington, Adams, Jefferson, Madison, Hamilton and Franklin—a journalist was known as a "newsmonger." This was not an insult; it was recognition of reality. A newsmonger sold news just as fishmonger sold fish. It was one more way to make a living

Now, just what was a fishmonger?

A fishmonger's daily task was to go down to the wharves and make a careful selection of the best fish he could find. A good fishmonger didn't simply pick any fish. He deliberately chose the fish that would sell best in the neighborhoods he served.

The fishmonger would then transport the fresh fish to his sales territory. He would sell the fish from a open-air stand in a market or from a cart that he would push along the city streets.

Whatever he failed to sell, he ate—either literally or financially. In those days before refrigeration, one either sold the fish that day, or lost the money he paid for the fish.

Now where did those fish come from? They didn't hop onto the docks. The fish arrived aboard ships from the open sea, where skilled fishermen used their knowledge, their instincts and their nets to catch the fish most likely to sell to the fishmongers.

If the fishmongers needed flounder, the fisherman came back with flounder. His job, his means of survival, was to catch the fish that the fishmonger would buy to resell to his customers.

Today, the news works in much the same way.

The mass media are today's newsmongers. They shop for news that will attract large audiences. They know what their audiences want and they are not interested in news that will not sell. They need fresh news everyday, just as the fishmongers needed fresh fish.

Now, where does all that news come from? Unlike the fishmongers, the media sometimes catch their own product by covering events (such as car crashes and council meetings) or through enterprise reporting (such as human-interest stories and investigative pieces).

But if you pay careful attention to the news media, particularly to newspapers, you will notice that the largest and most reliable supply of news items comes from the world of PR.

Consider these common stories:

- The federal government orders a recall of a brand-name product.

- A Blue Chip company reports it will exceed expectations on quarterly earnings.

- A medical research team says it has located the human gene that causes a common disorder.

Each of these stories, and hundreds of others, are brought to the newsmongers every day by PR specialists.

Journalists hate to admit this. They would prefer that readers and viewers believe that every story in the media came from the sweat off the brow of a hard-working reporter. But anytime you see verbs like "announced" or "revealed" in a news lead, you can bet the story came from a PR source.

PR specialists are the fishers who provide the product for the newsmonger. We sail the open waters of the business world, using our knowledge, our instincts and our wits to capture news that we know the newsmongers will find attractive.

The relationship is symbiotic. The newsmonger needs the PR pro just as badly as the PR pro needs the newsmonger.

Understanding and exploiting this turbulent relationship is the essence of PR Rainmaking.

I.e The Three Basic Rules of PR Rainmaking

To fully exploit this relationship, you must understand and apply these three rules:

1. Treat reporters like your customers.

2. Stack the odds in your favor.

3. Think "news," not "publicity."

The First Rule:
Treat Reporters Like Your Customers

1.1 Marketing Your News to the Media

If you want create a PR campaign that is effective and consistent, you must learn to market your story to the news media. You must learn to treat reporters as the customers who will either buy or reject your product: raw news.

Any effective PR Rainmaking campaign is grounded in three fundamental ideas:

a. The reporter is the consumer.

b. The story is the product that must be tailored for and sold to that consumer.

c. Reporters will buy your story for their reasons, not yours.

1.1a The Reporter is the Consumer

Today's PR specialists often forget this basic principle. The bad ones—the ones that reporters ridicule as mere "flacks"—never learn it.

To some of these folks, the reader or the viewer is their primary consumer. Others consider their client or their CEO to be the consumer of their work.

Wrong.

The PR Rainmaker knows: When it comes to getting your story into the media, you must look upon the reporter as your consumer.

Without the reporter, nothing happens. There is no story for your target audience to view or to read. There is nothing for your CEO to show his directors. There is nothing for your sales team to hand out to prospects.

Without the reporter, all you have is an idea.

The reporter is the consumer. The reporter is the customer. And you must act accordingly.

Does this mean, "the customer is always right?" Of course not. But that tired old saw is never true in any line of business.

If a repeat customer walks into a tire store and demands a free set of all-weather white walls, is the customer right? Not at all.

If that same customer demands a free wheel alignment with the purchase of all-weather white walls, is the customer right? Only if the store manager wants to keep that customer's business.

The point is: When it comes to getting media attention, the reporter is your customer. And the customer is usually right, but only within reason.

For example: Let's say that you are a private company working on a news story with a reporter from the local business journal. Just before press time, the reporter calls to get some "additional information." She wants to know how much total revenue your company posted during its last fiscal year.

You explain that your company is private and does not disclose its financials. The reporter explains that it is the business journal's policy to include the most recent revenue figure from any company it profiles.

It's very simple: No revenue figure, no news story

As the "store manager," it's up to you to decide whether this customer's demands are reasonable.

Is it more important to get the story in the business journal or to shield your revenue figures from the public? Only you and your team can make that choice.

Whenever possible, you should err on the side of the reporter's wants and needs, just as you would with any customer.

1.1b The Story is the Product

It is not enough that you want to sell something. Countless enterprises have lost money trying to sell a product they wanted to sell and no one wanted to buy.

No matter what you produce, you must find a market that wants to purchase your product.

The same holds true when placing your story in the news media. The PR Rainmaker knows that the story is the product. The story must be tailored for the consumer, who is the reporter. Then it must be sold to that reporter.

This is where PR flacks lose their direction. They look up media relations as mass production. They want to build an assembly line. They want to crank out one press release after another, send out a blast fax, and read their story in the newspapers the next day.

By using these "spray and pray" techniques, a company may well generate media coverage. But that coverage is likely to be ineffective. The key messages will be distorted. The story will go to the wrong audiences. The company will receive no return on its investment other than some newspaper clippings and perhaps some videotape.

The PR Rainmaker knows: The best news stories are earned one by one.

The assembly-line approach rarely works well in media relations. Reporters do not like to buy "off the rack." Each wants a story of his own. Each demands a custom fit.

So it becomes the PR Rainmaker's job to take stock of a reporter's needs and wants. We must tailor the story to fit that reporter. Then we must take that product and sell it to the reporter. We must convince the reporter that our story solves the reporter's six basic problems (which we will detail later).

We keep in mind during every step of developing the campaign: The reporter is the consumer and the story is the product.

1.1c Reporters Buy for Their Reasons, Not Ours

It is not unusual to spend hours designing a story for a specific reporter, only to have the reporter reject the idea. This can become incredibly frustrating.

This is one reason why so many flacks resort to assembly-line, blast-fax methods. "Why should I bother?" they say. "Why not just send out a thousand press releases and hope someone somewhere picks up the story?"

But PR Rainmakers understand and accept the challenge of executing an effective campaign. They know that, when it comes to convincing a reporter to buy any particular story, failure is far more likely than success.

As with any sales prospect, a reporter is more apt to say no than yes, even when you have tailored the story especially for that reporter.

Why? Who knows?

Maybe the reporter is working on a seven-part investigative series and doesn't have time. Maybe the reporter is being moved to another news beat. Maybe the reporter is coming down with the flu. Maybe the reporter is going on vacation. Maybe the reporter is just a jerk.

Who knows? Who cares?

When the reporter says no, move on.

Don't argue. Don't rage. Don't resort to spray and pray.

Advance to the next proposal with the next reporter.

Reporters will buy for their reasons, not ours. Keep telling yourself this and you will have a much better chance of holding your temper, maintaining your sanity and placing more stories in the news media.

1.2 The Two Questions You Must Answer

When considering whether to write a story, a journalist always begins with two questions:

- What's new?

- Who cares?

The first point is obvious. If something isn't new, then it can't be news. Most folks understand this instinctively.

It is the second point that most people have trouble understanding. It isn't enough for your item to be new. To qualify as news, your story must appeal to a broad audience. It must have significance for other people, and lot of them.

For example, consider the Taliban, the former rulers of Afghanistan.

Before the Sept. 11, 2001, attacks on the World Trade Center and the Pentagon, few news media paid any attention whatsoever to the Taliban. After Sept. 11 and through the fall of the Afghan regime, the media couldn't get enough stories about the Taliban.

What changed to make this happen? It wasn't the Taliban. What changed were the media's attitudes toward the Taliban:

- What's new? Terrorists have attacked the United States and they are being harbored by the Taliban in Afghanistan.

- Who cares? Virtually everyone.

Those two questions pushed the Taliban to the forefront of every mainstream newspaper, magazine, TV news program, radio news program and Web news site in the world.

This is an extreme example, but it makes the point.

If you want a story in the mainstream media, your story idea must appeal to a well-defined audience. If you want your story to appear in a trade magazine for nanotech engineers, then your story idea must appeal to nanotech engineers. If you want your story to appear in a suburban weekly, then your idea must appeal to the geographical, provincial interests of that weekly's subscribers.

The PR Rainmaker knows: If you want the news media to write about you or your company, you must clearly and concisely answer the questions "What's new?" and "Who cares?"

1.3 Every Reporter Has Six Basic Problems

Like anyone at any job, every journalist faces the same basic set of challenges every day. For the journalist, there are six of these fundamental problems. They are:

1. Finding a Story—The reporter's job is to uncover stories, preferably ones that the competition is missing. Most reporters must meet an unwritten quota of stories within a given period.

At a daily newspaper, the reporter may be required to turn in one 800-word story, plus a handful of briefs, every day. At a business journal, the quota may be three 800-word stories per week, plus an industry column, plus a brief. At a television station, the quota may be five news segments per week, plus a weekend feature.

The formula changes from outlet to outlet, from medium to medium. But be assured, every reporter has to meet certain expectations to keep any job, and this includes producing a given number of stories during a certain period of time.

2. Gathering the Facts—It's not enough to have a story to tell. The reporter must also have the facts that support the story.

This is known as the 5W's and the H: who, what, when, where, why and how. Without the facts, it becomes impossible to tell the story.

By nature and by training, reporters are generalists. Few have specialized knowledge, other than how to convert a set of facts into an interesting, intriguing news story.

As a result, every reporter is like a graduate student who is cramming for a new exam every day. Reporters must learn the essential facts, arrange them into a coherent stream and master them long enough to sound as if they are experts.

3. Choosing the Angle—Once reporters have the story and the facts, they must make a crucial decision. What is the angle they will take to writing the story?

The angle is simply the format that the reporter will use to arrange the story into something the audience can recognize and understand.

Is this a hard news story for the front page? Is it a feature for the Sunday family section? Is it a brief? Is it a six-part investigation?

These are just a few of the angles that the reporter might take to any story.

The most common angle is the hard news angle. Something important has happened and here are the facts, arranged in order of importance. The vast majority of stories you will read, see or hear are told with the hard news angle. The hard news story is based in immediacy. It must be told now, or it will lose its value to audience.

The second most common angle is the feature, which tends to de-emphasize the timeliness of the story, preferring to focus on some other interesting aspect, such a human-interest angle. A feature is not based in immediacy. It can hold for a few days or even weeks without losing its impact.

Then there are the many, many minor angles, such as the interpretive piece or the consumer investigation. Don't worry about these. Just learn to recognize a hard news story from a feature story.

4. Identifying the Peg—A news story is different from an entry in an encyclopaedia. Both contain facts. But the news requires a reason for the facts to be told.

That reason is the peg.

Don't confuse the peg with the angle. The angle is the reporter's approach to the story. The peg is the reporter's excuse for telling the story.

For example, virtually any encyclopaedia contains an entry about tobacco. But the reporter can't pick up this entry and report it as news. The facts are there, but not the peg.

However, if this morning a star athlete announces he has developed a cancer from using chewing tobacco, suddenly the reporter has a peg—a reason—to write about tobacco.

Every news story, no matter the angle, must have a peg. Without it, there is no reason to write the story.

5. Making the Deadline—Every journalist is racing against time.

The TV news reporter is fighting a 3 p.m. deadline for the 6 p.m. broadcast. The magazine reporter must meet a deadline three months from now. The Web reporter faces a new deadline every few minutes.

The deadline is just that: The last possible moment when the reporter is allowed to file a story for print, broadcast or transmission.

Reporters who miss their deadlines lose their jobs.

6. Satisfying the Boss—Every story must interest at least two people before it sees light. Those people are the reporter and his editor.

If either one rejects the story, it is dead.

The Boss also sets the criteria for the reporters: What they can cover, what they can pursue, how they can write their stories, what angles they can take, which pegs are acceptable and when the deadline is due.

Make no mistake. You may never see The Boss. But the world of journalism is ruled by the editor, not the reporter.

These are the problems that face every reporter: Story, facts, angle, peg, deadline and editors.

The PR Rainmaker knows: If you can help reporters solve their problems, you can become their best friend. And therein lies great opportunity.

1.4 Solving the Reporter's Problems

A basic law of business says: "When a consumer has a problem, that's an opportunity." The same holds true when dealing with reporters.

All reporters face six basic problems every single workday. They must uncover stories. They must find facts to support their stories. They must identify an angle and a peg. They must meet a deadline. They must satisfy The Boss.

PR Rainmakers views these problems as opportunities. If we can solve these six problems, reporters will greet us with open arms.

So how do we solve these problems?

We learn to think like reporters.

We understand their needs, their desires and their fears.

We:

- Offer news to report. We keep our eyes and ears open for news in our field. When we come across news—even if it's merely a lead—we pass that nugget onto the reporter whose favor we must court. We constantly look for genuine news about our own company that will interest the reporter, and we pass that news along as well. We become a steady, reliable source of valuable information. No reporter has enough of these sources. There is always room in the Rolodex for one more.

- Package the facts. Reporters are like graduate students cramming for an exam. The test is today's story. They need as many relevant facts as they can get, so they can sort out those that apply from those that do not. If we have access to these facts, we offer to provide them to the reporter in whatever form the reporter finds most useful. Some want the facts boiled down into a simple summary. Others want the entire database. Ask, then give.

- Provide expert commentary. We make ourselves available to help the reporter work through stories that deal in our areas of expertise. We provide the opinions that reporters cannot generate on their own. We speak in plain English and avoid jargon. We take a strong position that readers will find compelling.

- Suggest news angles and news pegs. We know the difference between hard news and soft features. We look for pegs, those timely opportunities that give the reporter an excuse to write about our company, our industry, our work.

- Honor the deadline. When the reporter calls, we respond immediately. We know that a journalist rarely calls without a purpose. A deadline is looming. The reporter is in near-panic. Our help is requested and we provide it immediately. Now, not later. We know that it takes just one failure to return the reporter's phone call to remove our name from the Rolodex.

If we provide these solutions consistently, we will help the reporter with the biggest challenge of all. We will make the Boss happy.

The PR Rainmaker knows: If the Boss smiles, the reporter smiles. And we benefit.

1.5 How to Win a Reporter's Heart

Like all other humans, reporters are subject to the Law of Reciprocity. When they receive cooperation, they will give cooperation. When they receive loyalty, they will give loyalty. When they receive gifts, they will give gifts.

This is a very human norm that is rooted in our collective past, when reciprocity was a tool of survival.

And this is why most media outlets forbid their reporters from accepting gifts from the public, especially from news sources. The majority of media ban gifts that are valued over a certain limit, generally $25 or so. Almost all news media forbid travel junkets as well.

Editors and producers want no questions to arise concerning any reporter's fairness and accuracy. Thus, the ban on gifts.

But there remains one gift that reporters will gladly accept and the Boss will gladly encourage.

That gift is "the scoop."

The scoop is an exclusive, important story. It is a news item that lets the reporter to beat the competition. It can be anything from a tip that the city council may change the town charter to a document that shows a local CEO is engaged in illegal insider trading.

Any tidbit of information that leads to a scoop is always welcome in a newsroom. Indeed, providing a steady supply of scoops is the only way to win a reporter's heart.

Scoops are what allow reporters to move up in the ranks. Scoops are what allow newspaper editors and TV producers to keep their jobs. Scoops are what allow newspapers to attract more readers, TV stations to attract more viewers, radio stations to attract more listeners and Web sites to attract more hits.

The PR Rainmaker knows: Scoops allow us to bypass the media's ban on gifts and to tap into the reporter's natural desire to observe the Law of Reciprocity.

Become a valuable source, provide access to a steady stream of scoops, and you will receive more favorable coverage. It's human nature.

Reporters will succumb to the Law of Reciprocity. They will turn to you more often for expert commentary. They will look more favorably upon your story proposals.

In addition, reporters will succumb to the Law of Self-Interest. If you are providing scoops on a regular basis, a reporter is going to resist doing anything that might cause you to turn off the tap.

How frequent is a "steady" stream? One good tip per month is plenty.

If you are at all plugged into your industry or profession or community, you will hear plenty of good information to send along to the reporter.

Get in the habit of passing news along to the reporter just as soon as you hear it. Also, take the reporter to lunch once a month to exchange information. Always take along plenty of potential scoops, even if they are nothing more than tidbits or rumors that you have heard.

Every reporter wants an inside source, a "Deep Throat." It's all part of the romantic image that most reporters have about their jobs.

Two cautions about reporters and reciprocation:

1. Never expect immediate quid pro quo. Understand that your relationship with a reporter will grow over time. Don't rush the process. Accept that you will always put more into the relationship than you will get out. If the reporter suspects that you think he owes you something, your relationship will sour fast.

2. Reciprocation only goes so far. If you're a valuable source, and the reporter has the story that your company is a front for the Mob, don't expect a pass. It won't happen. Because of your relationship, you'll probably receive more courtesy than will the usual subject of a tough story. But that's all.

1.6 Offer the Reporter a Lay-down

The news media are filled with sharp, educated folks. The problem is, deadlines don't always give reporters time to sort out complex issues. Thus it is the PR Rainmaker's job to make everything about a story as simple as possible for the reporter.

Any story we propose should have the clear appearance of news. It should fit the reporter's needs. Every detail should be explained in simple, clear language.

As the American philosopher Henry David Thoreau said: "Simplify, simplify, simplify!"

In Texas, we play a domino game known as "Forty-Two", which is similar to bridge. What every Forty-Two player enjoys most is drawing a hand that wins before the first domino is played. This is known as a "lay-down." The player can literally turn the hand face up and every other player will see the hand is a winner.

Reporters also need lay-downs.

Every day, they must submit from two to four stories due to the Boss.

When you are under that kind of pressure, it's great to get a story proposal that is ready made for your needs. A lay-down not only offers a great story idea, but supplies the peg, the angle, the facts, the sources and the opposing view as well.

A story proposal like that is always welcome because it is simple to execute, yet fits every aspect of the reporter's criteria for news.

This level of simplicity is achieved only through hard work and high ingenuity on the part of the PR Rainmaker.

To better understand this level of simplicity, consider the most famous equation in science, Albert Einstein's $E=mc^2$.

The equation is simple. It says that energy (E) is the same as any mass (m) that is propelled to the speed of light (c^2). In other words, energy and mass are the same thing, but exist at different speeds.

From this simple equation, Einstein explained an incredible number of observations. Indeed, Einstein turned the science of physics upside down.

This is what made Einstein a genius: His ability to take the most complex thoughts and reduce them to a simple, useful equation that others could understand and put to use.

If you want to be a PR Rainmaker, you must also strive to make the complex as simple as possible.

Offer the reporter a lay-down. Be prepared to spoon-feed your story to the news media.

If you do, you will improve your ability to place stories in the news media. Plus, those stories will more accurately reflect your intentions and will better serve your needs.

1.7 Make the Reporter a Player

Reporters live for scoops. Their days are consumed with a relentless search for news they can break.

Scoops are what separate successful reporters from also-rans. Scoops lead to awards. Scoops lead to raises. Scoops lead to promotions. Scoops lead to better jobs at bigger media.

Thus, who is the reporter's best friend? A source who consistently helps that reporter beat his competition to important news.

But why stop at being a friend? If you help that reporter become a player, then you become family.

The PR Rainmaker knows: There's no better way to put a reporter in your pocket than to become that reporter's connection to the inner sanctums of power and influence.

Your first step is to identify a reporter who covers your industry as a beat. A "beat" is simply the category where the reporter is assigned to find news. A reporter who covers the mayor and the city council is on the "city hall beat." A reporter who writes about crime is on the "cop beat."

Business reporters also cover beats, often more than one. These are usually broken down by industry, and tend to reflect your city's economy. Generally, most city dailies will have reporters who cover finance, retail, restaurants, real estate, transportation and health care. Some will also cover technology, tourism, law, not-for-profits and other such areas.

The easiest way to find out which reporter covers your industry is to simply call the business editor and ask. Another way is to read stories written about your industry and take note of the bylines. The reporter who writes most often about your sector probably owns that beat.

The next step is to make of list of the power brokers in your industry. Don't stop at the high profile players. Think long and hard to identify those executives and professionals who may not make headlines, but who have great influence nonetheless.

Ask around. Make sure your list is complete.

Once you are certain you have a complete list, check off the names of the power brokers who know you by name and by sight. Then focus on getting to know the others on your list. You don't have to become best friends with these power brokers. You just have to be able to call them on the phone and speak to them in a comfortable, friendly way.

Most executives are willing to network freely as long as you are not obviously trying to sell them something. Take them to lunch. Join their clubs. Play golf with them. Keep it light and make no demands.

Now it's time to bring the reporter into your world.

Start by making the initial contact. Ask the reporter to lunch. Make it clear you don't have a story to sell. Instead, identify yourself as someone who knows the reporter's beat and who is willing to be a source.

A reporter never has enough sources.

Be persistent without being obnoxious. Reporters aren't always the most social animals. They don't always return the first phone call, not because they are louts, but because they are consumed with making their next deadline and may fear wasting time on a dead end.

The key to getting the reporter to call you back is to immediately demonstrate your value.

If you hear some news you think the reporter may not know, call it in.

Also, read the reporter's stories. If you can help with information or background, say so.

If you consistently supply material the reporter can use, you will get a lunch date.

Once that happens, you want to advance steadily from serving as a source to serving as a mentor. Ask the reporter about the beat. Who does the reporter want to meet? What does the reporter want to know?

Then put that information to work. Offer to introduce the reporter to the industry's key players. Drop a name or two, again without being obnoxious or obvious.

Few reporters will turn down a chance to get to know the power broker who have proven inaccessible.

Will the power broker meet with the reporter? Almost always, if it is clear that the meeting is not an interview, but rather a "getting to know you" session. No notepads, no probing questions.

The idea is to make a connection and nothing more. Some reporters, particularly young ones, will not understand this unless you carefully explain it.

Keep the first meeting as informal as possible. Make it over a meal, or over drinks, or over a round of golf. Your only job is to make the introduction and to break the ice. What happens after that is up to the reporter and the power broker.

As your alliance with the reporter grows, so will your opportunities to shape and to mold that reporter. Offer insights. Invite the reporter to insider events. Show the reporter your industry from the inside out.

Most of all, tip off the reporter to any breaking news you know about, unless doing so would violate a responsibility.

Providing scoops raises your value. They put the reporter in your debt.

Does this mean the indebted reporter can and will do anything for you? Not at all. The reporter must answer to an editor. The reporter has a set of rules to follow.

But an indebted reporter will return your calls promptly. An indebted reporter will bend over backwards to help you.

Suppose an indebted reporter refuses to recognize the debt and treats you indifferently. Then put on the squeeze. Vanish for a month or so. Ignore the reporter's phone calls. Shut the reporter out of your world long enough for the supply of scoops to dry up. Only then renew contact, making some excuse that you were out of town or buried under a mountain of work.

Make the reporter feel the debt. If the reporter has any brains at all, the pain of separation should make your point.

One other thing you must realize: Good reporters move onward and upward. Few remain on the same beat for more than a year or two. They get promoted. They find better jobs.

Always be ready to train the next beat reporter. Make the contact as early as possible. Be the new reporter's guide to the beat. Make yourself indispensable and you will prosper.

The PR Rainmaker knows: If you want to create an ally in the news media, you must transform a reporter into a player.

The Second Rule:
Stack the Odds in Your Favor

2.1 Study What Works and Copy It

Flacks take the approach, "Let's throw all the spaghetti against the wall and see what sticks."

Reject that notion now.

PR Rainmakers are constantly looking for ways to improve their odds of attracting positive attention from the news media. They study individual reporters and editors. They analyze individual publications, broadcasts and Web sites.

They take the time to understand the news media and how they react to specific circumstances. They understand the reporter's problems and they solve them.

They look for ways to stack the odds in their favor.

Dealing with the media is a lot like gambling in Las Vegas. The odds are always against your placing any particular story. Far more news releases end up in the garbage than find a place in the newspaper or on the television.

But there are ways to improve your chances. In gambling, you do this by studying the odds and playing accordingly. The same is true in PR Rainmaking. You study what works, then you apply what you learn.

Anytime you deal with the news media, you want to stack the odds in your favor. You will need every advantage you can get.

2.2 Play 'Tight and Aggressive'

Poker will teach you more about human nature that just about any activity short of physical combat.

Greed versus fear. Risk versus reward. Truth versus deception. You can find it all in a late night session of Texas Hold 'Em.

There are two basis approaches to playing poker. One type of player believes that victory is possible with any hand, if you know how to read your fellow players and how to skillfully execute a bluff. The other believes in waiting for a certain combination of cards that indicate a high probability of victory, then betting aggressively on those strong hands.

In Texas Hold 'Em, you receive just two cards before placing your first bet. The best players will avoid betting at all unless those first two cards are strong cards. They will bet only if they have some combination of aces, kings, queens, jacks or tens, or if they draw a pair.

Anything less, and they fold their hand.

This strategy is called "tight and aggressive."

It's tight, because the player will bet only in very specific circumstances. It's aggressive, because (once the player gets the combination he wants) he plays hard to win, giving up only when it becomes obvious that another player has a stronger hand.

2.2a How the Amateurs Play

When dealing with reporters, PR flacks and their clients play as if they can win with any hand they are dealt.

They begin with some vague notion that they have a bit of news that someone out there is eagerly waiting to publish. So the flacks hammer out a press release, which passes through a committee that usually includes the top executives and the legal staff.

If the release contained any real news value before it went to this committee, it is now buried under a pile of ego and adjectives. Next, the flacks transmit the release to a long list of media outlets, not bothering to target any specific reporter or editor, hoping the information will find its way into the right hands.

They are then shocked when their story idea finds few takers.

They are playing a loose game of PR, betting on any hand and hoping to bluff their way to victory. They play like amateurs.

2.2b The Two Cards You Must Have in Your Hand

PR Rainmakers play "tight and aggressive." Like the professional poker player in a game of Texas Hold 'Em, PR Rainmakers insist upon having certain cards in their hands before placing a bet.

These cards are:

1. Newsworthiness.

2. Timeliness.

If you want to create a story that will appeal to a journalist, you must begin with both of these cards in your hand.

Without newsworthiness or without timeliness, you should fold your hand. You have little chance at victory. There is no point in betting your time, money and effort trying to bluff your way to a win. The odds are stacked too heavily against you.

2.2c What is Newsworthiness?

First, to be newsworthy the story must have significant impact upon the news audience. The fact that the story interests you, or your client, or your CEO is irrelevant. This qualifies the story only for your company newsletter.

To qualify for the news media, the story must interest readers, viewers or listeners. If you want to place a story in an engineering trade magazine, then your story must interest a broad range of engineers. If you want to place your story in USA Today, then your story must interest a broad range of the general public.

Second, to be newsworthy your story must identify a conflict, signal a change, deal with a problem or point out an oddity. We will detail these four elements in a later chapter. Suffice it to say: A story that lacks at least one of these elements, by definition, cannot be newsworthy.

2.2d What is Timeliness?

To satisfy the need for timeliness, you must provide the reporter with a news peg: a reason to tell your story right now.

Before Sept. 11, 2001, there was little interest in the news media in the Taliban. After Sept. 11, that lack of interest turned into a frenzy of interest.

What changed? The story became timely.

The Taliban issue had developed a news peg. There was now a reason to tell the story.

That's an extreme example, but the lesson holds in any story situation. It's not news that Xerox hired a new CEO two years ago. It is news that Xerox will get a new CEO this afternoon. The difference is timeliness.

By definition, news is timely. If you can't tie your story to breaking news, or at least to very recent events, then shelve the story. Your best bet is to wait for a future event will make your story timely once again.

2.2e Never Bet on a Weak Hand

PR Rainmakers play "tight and aggressive" at all times. They never let ego, emotion or outside pressure push them into betting on a losing hand.

They insist that every story they take to the news media include two essential cards: newsworthiness and timeliness.

2.3 Put on your game FACE

Every news story must have a FACE. If your forget to put a FACE on your story proposal, your chances of interesting a reporter are nil.

By FACE, the PR Rainmaker means:

- F: Feelings

- A: Analysis

- C: Crisis

- E: Energy

These are the elements of a well-crafted story proposal. Let's look at each part one by one.

Feelings are the emotions that your story stirs within the reporter, and thus the reader. The seven basic emotions are love, hate, anger, fear, sorrow, envy and greed. There are endless degrees, combinations and variations on these seven. (For example, "pity" is fear blended with sorrow. "Rage" is an extreme form of "anger."). Your story must strongly arouse one, and only one, of these basic emotions. (Note that only one of these emotions, "love," is positive. This is one reason why news is almost always negative.)

Analysis provides the logic that sells the story. Feelings open the door with a reporter, but logic closes the sale. Analysis may come in the form of numbers, statistics, data, studies, surveys or expert commentary. The key is that the analysis must at least appear to be objective and accurate. The analysis allows reporters to take your story seriously. It also gives reporters a subconscious excuse to listen to their feelings.

Crisis is the inherent conflict within the story. Without conflict, there is no news. This is what reporters mean when they talk about getting "both sides of the story." Every story must have at least two sides. Ideally, for the news media, the story has a hero on one side and a villain on the other. You want to be the hero.

Energy is what results from mixing feelings, analysis and crisis in the right proportions. Energy is what drives the story. It is what compels the reporter to want to write the story. It is what compels the editor to give the story good play. It is what compels the reader to finish the story, to remember your story, to pass it along to friends.

The PR Rainmaker knows: You never take on the media without putting on your game FACE.

2.4 Write Proposals, Not Releases

There are only two times to write a news release.

The first is when your story is so big that your only real problem is finding a room large enough to hold all the reporters who want to attend your press conference.

The other is when your news is so small that it warrants only the briefest mention.

The first instance is rare and is generally reserved for large-cap public companies. Microsoft announces that Bill Gates is stepping down as CEO. Coca-Cola announces a settlement in a yearlong racial discrimination suit. Ford announces it is recalling thousands of Explorers to replace their Firestone tires. These are examples of when a press release is the right choice.

The second instance is fairly common and is found in organizations of all kinds: public, private, governmental and not-for-profit. Your organization names a new vice president. Your company announces its second-quarter profits. Such news is condensed into a release and distributed to local newspapers and trade magazines, usually with solid results.

But all too often a CEO expects the mainstream media and the trade press to jump on a story that simply has no obvious news value.

A prominent restaurant chain opens its second location in a major city. The first location got great coverage; the second should get even more, right?

Wrong.

There's no obvious news value to a second location. Send that as a news release to the media, and your story will line garbage cans throughout your town.

The PR Rainmaker knows: In most situations, it is better to think in terms of proposals, not releases.

Instead of releasing a general idea to the media at-large, tailor your story to specific reporters at specific publications.

Forget the headline: "Restaurant Opens Second Great Location."

Consider breaking your one large story into several smaller stories, then selling the pieces to the media one at a time.

Does your new restaurant offer a trendy new dish or an exotic cocktail? Call the local morning show producers and offer to show viewers how to make it at home.

Installing a high-tech kitchen with a flash-cook oven unlike any other in town? Call the restaurant-beat writer at the local business journal and offer an exclusive look at how the device will make your restaurant among the most profitable in town.

Is your celebrity investor dropping in to check out your site? Take high-quality photos and send them to the city's gossip columnist. Better yet, call the talk radio station and offer a live interview.

If nothing else, plan a stunt. Break a world record. Get outrageous.

But forget about mailing, faxing or e-mailing a news release.

Propose your stories one at a time. That's how the PR Rainmaker works.

2.5 Change the Customer, Not the Product

When faced with customers who are either ignoring or abandoning their products, CEOs often choose to alter their products to fit demand. This is usually a path to disaster.

Altering a product is expensive and time-consuming, eating away at precious resources and profits. It also damages the strength of its brand name, confusing the consumer and widening the rift.

The PR Rainmaker understands that there are two ways of doing business. You can compete or you can create.

Most companies compete for the same set of customers. In a growing market, this works just fine. The number of available customers is going up and up, so there's plenty for anyone who is willing to get out there and fight for them.

But what happens when a market refuses to grow? Or worse, what happens when a market actually begins to shrink. Suddenly, you are fighting for fewer and fewer customers. Your pricing power vanishes. So do your profits.

Instead, companies should seek to change the customer by creating new behaviors. The best method for this is public relations.

No one understood this better than Edward L. Bernays, the father of modern PR. Indeed, according to Bernays, it is this principle of changing the public instead of the product that separates PR from advertising and marketing.

Whenever hired to sell a product to the consumer, Bernays always chose to sell a new behavior instead.

He began by quickly analyzing the public behavior that prevented his client from thriving. He then determined how the public would need to think and to act in order to benefit his client.

Finally, Bernays would select the strategy and the tactics that would alter public opinion and consumer behavior to fit his needs.

2.5a Caution: Bernays at Work

His methods were indirect, complex and at times inscrutable. They employed front organizations, public demonstrations, letter-writing campaigns, expert testimony and other alliances.

But more often than not, they worked:

- Assigned to sell books for Simon & Schuster, Bernays enlisted experts to call for great literature in the everyday home, plus he convinced architects to include built-in bookshelves in their home designs.

- Called in to bolster the sagging luggage industry, Bernays persuaded colleges to inform their freshman students about the wide array of suitcases they would need on campus. He also hired singer Eddie Cantor to pose for magazine photos while packing a large trunk for a coming tour.

- When the hairnet industry found itself threatened by the shorter hairstyles of the 1920s, Bernays convinced health officials to require restaurant employees to wear hairnets. He also urged fashion setters and famous artists to write newspaper articles that proclaimed the beauty of long, flowing hairstyles.

- When Proctor & Gamble found that it couldn't get children to use Ivory Soap, Bernays organized national soap-carving contests for kids.

- When the bacon industry found itself being shut out of the urban American breakfast during the Roaring Twenties, Bernays found doctors to proclaim that a "hearty breakfast" of bacon and eggs is more healthful than a light breakfast of coffee, fruit and toast.

The key, Bernays said, is to get a credible champion to say what you need to have said or to do what you need to have done in order to alter the public's opinion. Bernays would build an event around this champion's words or actions, thus attracting media attention.

In this way, he would change the opinions and behaviors of consumers, and thus grow the overall market for his clients.

Bernays knew what many CEOs forget: It is always better to own a small share of a growing market than a large share of a shrinking market.

2.5b Three Steps to Changing the Customer

The Bernays Formula for employing the news media to change public behavior is simple, but effective:

1. Use PR to generate an event.

2. Use the event to generate news.

3. Use the news to change opinion or behavior.

Of course, today's news media are far more skeptical than they were in Bernays' day. But they are just as easily manipulated by the PR Rainmaker who has the creativity and the moxie to put Bernays' ideas to work.

Don't believe it?

Study the media machinations of the Clinton White House.

Observe the techniques of activist groups opposing everything from old-growth forestry to global trade.

Dissect the news in national media and look for the front groups, the third-party experts and the public events that are used to mold public opinion.

You can apply these same techniques today to grow your business.

The PR Rainmaker knows what Bernays knew: If you want to attract more customers or clients, focus on changing their opinions and behaviors, not on changing your product or service.

Or, as Napoleon told his generals, "Circumstance? I make circumstance."

2.6 Be a Hero, Not a Zero

Every company has a choice. It can be a hero, a villain or a zero.

The PR Rainmaker always chooses to portray his company as a hero as quickly and as effectively as possible.

Being a hero automatically translates into solid reputation and high credibility.

Solid reputation translates into new customers and clients. High credibility can delay, avert or even prevent a future media crisis.

Becoming a hero is a process that must begin immediately. If you wait, your company may end up like Exxon in the wake of the Valdez oil spill in 1989. More than a decade later, Exxon still suffers from its portrayal in the news media as a villain, thanks largely to the ineptitude of its CEO and its PR machine.

Exxon does a lot of great work in its community. For example, the company spends big money to save endangered tigers through zoo management and research.

It doesn't matter.

Exxon could cure cancer, and yet an entire generation will always link Exxon with the Valdez oil spill. Exxon is a media villain, typecast as certainly as the Sheriff of Nottingham and the Wicked Witch of the West.

No PR effort can save the Exxon brand. It's too late. It is a villain and can never become a hero. (Want proof? A 2001 survey of executives named Exxon-Mobil as the least attractive CEO job in the nation.)

Exxon's mistake was to adopt the strategy that is adopted by most companies out of fear or ignorance: To portray themselves as zeroes. These companies want to appear entirely neutral. They want to around no strong feelings from the public by engaging in any crusade that would transform their brand from a zero into a hero.

At first glance, being a zero appears to be the safe choice.

This was the position adopted by chemical maker W.R. Grace before the book and the movie "A Civil Action," by the investment firm Drexel Lambert before the junk bond scandals of the late 1980s and by Union Carbide before a gas cloud killed 1,400 people in Bhopal, India.

All three brands are now villain brands because the companies failed to move themselves from zero to hero in the public mind.

As with Exxon, it is too late to save W.R. Grace, Drexel Lambert and Union Carbide from being portrayed as villains.

Don't fall into the zero trap.

PR Rainmakers portray their companies as heroes before the news media can use a crisis to turn their companies into villains. We will discuss how in the coming chapters.

2.7 Start at the Top

Begin at the bottom rung of the news media and work your way to the top. That's the conventional wisdom most companies follow.

PR specialists call this "building credibility."

This approach sees the media as something like the farm systems used in professional baseball during the mid-20th century.

Back then, a prospect went straight from high school to Single-A ball. If the prospect mastered that level of minor league baseball, he moved up to Double-A, then Triple-A.

And if the player proved his skills at Triple-A, maybe…just maybe…he would get an invitation to play Major League Baseball.

This is the concept that many PR specialists sell to their clients.

"We'll begin with the trade publications and the small newspapers," they say. "Once we build our credibility there, we can move up to the daily newspapers and to large-market television. And if we succeed there, maybe…just maybe…we can break in with the national media. This will take years of hard work, but we can get you there if you trust us and do as we say."

Bull.

The PR Rainmaker knows: Start at the top.

Put all of your resources initially into breaking your story in the Big Media. Focus on the national newspapers—The New York Times, The Wall Street Journal, USA Today, The Los Angeles Times—and on the regional newspapers that serve the top 20 markets, such as the Boston Globe, the Chicago Tribune or The Dallas Morning News.

There is sound thinking behind this tactic.

2.7a One Good Key Will Open Many Gates

One story in a major publication will do more for your reputation than will a thousand stories in lesser publications.

Get you name into the Wall Street Journal, and you achieve instant credibility with just about any other media you contact.

Gates that were closed to you will suddenly spring wide open.

Why?

The rest of the media hate to admit this, but the major daily newspapers still set the agenda for national debate. If a story appears in the New York Times, then reporters, editors and producers across the nation know that the story has met the most stringent of journalistic standards.

This gives journalists a sense of comfort that most of them secretly crave. Think of it as journalism's version of The Good Housekeeping Seal of Approval.

For all their bombast about their independence, only a very few reporters, editors and producers are mavericks. Journalists are far more comfortable running in packs than flying solo. They care very much about how they are viewed by their peers. (Thus the obsession with the Pulitzer Prize and other awards.)

Think back to the movie "All the President's Men," which is a remarkably accurate portrayal of the Washington Post's efforts to break open the Watergate scandal of the Nixon White House.

There's a scene midway through the movie where the editors are debating whether to continue the investigation. If this story is so big, they ask one another, why are we the only news outlet in the entire nation that is covering it?

Editors, reporters and producers ask each other this question every day.

If Time magazine is running a cover story about the White House, you can bet the editors at Newsweek and U.S. News are asking each other, "Why didn't we have a cover story about the White House?" If CNN sends a reporter to cover a hurricane in Puerto Rico, you can bet producers at CBS, ABC and NBC will ask, "Why don't we have a reporter in Puerto Rico?"

And if a story appears in a national newspaper, you can bet other news media will at least consider producing their own version of the story. It terrifies them to do otherwise.

2.7b No Company is Too Small for National Attention

Resolve that you will start at the top, then work your way down. Understand that getting that first story in the Big Media will be exhausting and frustrating. But also realize that, once you land your national story, your other PR efforts will become many times more effective.

"But we can't do that," you may be telling yourself. "My company is too small. We lack the clout to get the Big Media to pay attention to us."

The PR Rainmaker knows: The Big Media care only about the story, not the size of the company behind the story.

Journalists just want a good tale to tell. It doesn't matter to them whether your company is large or small, whether you are a Nobel laureate or a small-town dogcatcher. They just want a good story.

With some knowledge, skill and creativity, you can provide them with a good story.

Is it easier for a major corporation to get media coverage than it is for a start-up? To a certain extent, yes. A big company like Microsoft has a massive PR budget and scores of PR specialists at its disposal. It can crank out an endless series of media releases, press conferences, photo ops and news junkets.

But study a week's worth of the New York Times, The Wall Street Journal and USA Today. Devote a week to watching the networks' morning and evening news programs as well as their news magazines. Note how often you see, hear and read about companies and individuals you've never seen, heard or read about before.

You can be among them. PR Rainmaking will get you there.

Do yourself a big favor. Don't waste time, energy and money "building credibility" in the minor leagues.

When you're ready to roll, start at the top.

2.8 Always Have a Plan B

PR Rainmakers know they can do everything right, and still fail to make news.

It's a fact of life. Accept it now.

All news is affected by whatever else happened that day. All news is relative.

Newspapers have only so many columns to fill. The TV news has only so many minutes to devote. Even Web sites have only so many slots to fill with news of the day.

Even on a slow news day, more copy is thrown away than is ever used. More emails are deleted than followed. More faxes are trashed than considered.

There is also a hierarchy to news, especially in the mainstream media. Breaking news will supplant soft news, such as features and analyses. News of broad interest will supplant news of specific interest; for example, a tornado that wipes out your downtown area will likely push a local school board meeting to the back pages, if not out of newspaper entirely.

You can arrange the most visual, most intriguing media event possible. But if City Hall is burning down at the same time as your event, then that is where the news cameras are going to go. The news demands it.

We all know what happened on Sept. 11, 2001: Two passenger jets slammed into the World Trade Center, while a third crashed into the Pentagon and a fourth was forced to the ground in a Pennsylvania field.

Just think how many important and interesting news events were chased out of the news media on Sept. 11 and during the weeks that followed—not to mention all of the soft news features and media events that were canceled.

So how do PR Rainmakers handle this reality? By leaving nothing to chance.

In others words: Always have a Plan B.

- Keep the time window for your media event as open as long as is reasonably possible. If you arrange for a media event to last only one hour, then you severely limit the media's ability to attend. You may force the media to choose between your event and breaking news. If you force that choice, you will lose. Keep the window open for at least three hours. If the participants (such as the CEO), balk at this idea, ask them bluntly: "How badly do you want to be in the news?" The media are in control of whether you get coverage, not you.

- Choose a time that will work best for the news media. Generally, the best time for any event is between 10 a.m. and 2 p.m. on Monday, Tuesday, Wednesday and Thursday. These are the times when the news media have the most resources available to cover events. These windows also give the reporters plenty of time to meet their deadlines.

- Have your video crew on standby. Almost any city will have a company that provides video services for a variety of needs. Arrange to have a crew on standby, ready to step into the situation if breaking news draws the media away. Your crew members can shoot video and audio of the event, just as if they were the news media. They can then edit the raw footage into what is known as a "B roll," which is a videotape of event highlights that you can provide to the local media. You must move quickly. Shoot the footage, prepare the B roll and get it to the TV stations on deadline. You cannot wait for tomorrow.

- Be prepared to move to another date. When designing a media event, be sure to compare the event date with other events around the city. Avoid conflicts whenever possible. Monitor the news media as your event approaches. Have a back-up date in mind, in case other events threaten to eclipse your own. And if the newsworthiness of your event is threatened, especially by breaking news, do not hesitate to make the change.

PR Rainmakers understand and accept they are not fully in control. They know the daily news is driven by immediate events, not by advanced planning.

The only insurance policy is a sound Plan B.

2.9 Every Reporter Wants a Pulitzer

Whenever you deal with the news media, there is a primary rule that you must keep in mind at all times.

This is Cawley's Theorem of Media Relations:

1. All journalists secretly believe they will someday win the Pulitzer Prize.

2. No journalist ever won the Pulitzer by writing nice things about American business.

Therefore: If a journalist finds out something negative about your company, expect to see it in the news.

So what's the point of this theorem?

Anytime you deal with a journalist—whether in person, online, by phone, by letter, in a media kit, whatever—realize you are dealing with a tiger.

The tiger may purr. The tiger may preen. The tiger may even run and jump and play. But if the tiger smells fresh meat, the tiger will feed.

No matter how friendly you become with a journalist, no matter how well an interview goes, no matter how warm and fuzzy you feel as you wait for a story to appear: Expect negatives.

The journalist's job is not to make your company look good. The journalist's job is to report an intriguing story that an editor will approve, an audience will read and—if possible—a prize committee will recognize with praise and trophies.

And nothing makes a story more intriguing than a big, fat, hairy, embarrassing negative.

Let's put it this way: The Washington Post's Bob Woodward didn't become Bob Woodward by writing nice stories. He spent the early part of his career digging up as many embarrassing stories about government agencies and private companies as he could. He cut his teeth by revealing corporate greed and government waste.

Then came Watergate, which gave Woodward the opportunity to apply all his well-honed, field-tested skills to dismantling the Nixon administration.

This is how a suburban beat reporter becomes Bob Woodward.

So:

- If a reporter tours your job site before a groundbreaking ceremony, and sees a laundry list of OSHA violations, expect the violations to appear in the story.

- If a reporter visits your headquarters to profile your CEO, and happens to view a layoff order on an assistant's desk, expect to see the layoff reported in the news media.

- If a reporter attends a preview of your newest product, and comes across a consumer advocate who believes your product is a threat to public health, expect to see the advocate's comments prominently played in the article.

The point of Cawley's Theorem is not to make you fearful of the news media. The point is to make you keenly aware that there is risk as well as reward in dealing with reporters.

You cannot control what the reporter reports. You must deal with this basic truth. Your CEO must deal with it. Your entire company culture must deal with it.

Like the rest of us, journalists are looking to advance in their careers. There's no faster way to advance in journalism than by winning the Pulitzer.

And you win the Pulitzer with brass-knuckle reporting.

The PR Rainmaker always keeps in mind: The reporter is never your friend and is never looking out for your best interests.

The Third Rule:
Think 'News,' Not 'Publicity'

3.1 The Story Idea is Everything

You can do everything else right.

You can craft a superb media list. You can write a news release that makes your boss do cartwheels. You can design a breathtaking press kit.

But you have don't have a story that interests the news media, what difference does any of that make?

On the other hand, you can slap together a half-ass media list, you can whip out a sloppy release and you can drop your press documents into a plastic shopping bag for delivery.

And if you have a great news story to tell, you will still get the news media to pay attention to you.

It happens every day. Amateurs consistently match or even beat professional publicists simply because they spend more time creating the news than in creating media accessories.

Too many PR specialists—both in agencies and in corporations—put far too much emphasis on the icing and not enough on the cake. The icing is the media list, the news release and the press kit. The cake is the news story.

Why do they do this? Because cooking up a solid news story requires discipline. It also requires thoughtfulness, boldness and creativity. Most of all, it requires the raw nerve of looking the boss and the bureaucracy in the eye and saying, "It ain't news yet."

PR Rainmakers know: In the world of news, the story is all that really matters. If you offer real news, the news media will do the rest for you.

For this reason, PR Rainmakers put invest their energy into fashioning a story that the news media will eagerly accept. They resist the urge to give the CEO a nod and a smile and a quick yes.

They are willing to say: "Not yet."

Why? Because PR Rainmakers understand quite clearly that, if the media ignores their company's story, the blame will fall squarely upon the PR department's shoulders.

The story is everything. The story is all.

That is why PR Rainmakers never think, "Let's get some publicity." Instead, they insist upon answering the question, "What is our story?"

To get the news media's attention, you must create news.

To create news, you must think "news," not "publicity."

It's just that damn simple.

3.2 Performance Comes Before Publicity

Far too often, the CEO calls the publicist and says, "Get us some media coverage." All too seldom does the CEO stop to think, "What do we have to offer that the media would want to cover?"

The PR Rainmaker knows: Before you can attract a reporter, you must have something for to report. It doesn't get any more basic than that. And yet so many executives, professionals and entrepreneurs fail to comprehend this simple fact.

Instead, they have their publicist call the reporter and say something along these lines: "We have a great company and a terrific CEO. Are you interested in doing a story on us?"

Reporters hear this sort of lame pitch day in, day out. And you know what? It rarely works. When it does work, it is because the journalist is very inexperienced or was already interested in your company before you called.

Beware of either situation.

An inexperienced journalist is as likely to get your story wrong as right and will probably churn out an article that will get poor play and little readership.

A journalist who is interested in your company before you call probably has an agenda in mind. Odds are this journalist will discard your message and focus on that agenda while pretending to deeply care about what you have to say.

Publicity is not advertising. It is not a product or a service for you to buy. You cannot place an order. You cannot dictate content. You are not in control.

You must negotiate for publicity with those who are in control: the news media.

And that means you must give a good reporter a reason to report about your company. You must be newsworthy. You must perform.

3.3 So What Exactly Is News?

If you watch TV news or read a newspaper, and pay careful attention what is presented to you, you will find that every story contains at least one of four elements.

These are change, conflict, aberration and problem.

Some stories will contain more than one of these elements. Generally speaking, the more elements within the story, the stronger the story.

For example, if the story is about your town tearing down City Hall, that's change. If the local preservation society protests the destruction, that's conflict. If your City Hall is the first to be torn down in your state in 50 years, that's aberration. And if, underneath the wrecked City Hall, your local government finds a toxic waste dump, that's a problem.

You can see how a story that contains all four elements is more interesting—and thus stronger—than one that contains only one or two elements.

The PR Rainmaker knows: The more elements you include in your story proposal, the more likely a reporter will see your story as news.

3.3a What is Change?

Change is the most common form of news. Your company hires a new chief executive. Your company opens a new manufacturing plant. Your company launches a new product line.

Because change is the most common element, it is also the weakest. Change alone will seldom get the attention of a journalist.

3.3b What is Conflict?

Conflict, on the other hand, is the strongest of the four elements. Not because it is rare, but because it is emotional.

Journalists like to talk about reasoned and balanced reporting. But the fact is that TV, newspapers, magazines and radio love to cover a good scrap.

Think for a second about the journalist's creed to "tell both sides of the story." What does this promise imply? That there is a conflict within every story.

Indeed, journalists will go to extremes to find "the other side," even when it doesn't exist. Why? Because if they don't, they can expect rebuke from an editor or a producer who will demand to know, "Why are you only telling one side of the story?"

If you want your story proposal to get noticed, you will need to build in a conflict, even if it is a minor one.

3.3c What is Aberration?

The local man who has hiccuped continuously for 25 years. The 10-cent stamp that is sold at auction for $1.5 million. The international survey that shows Americans think about sex more often than any other national groups. These are aberrations.

They are the off-beat, off-kilter, even goofy stories that you will find at the end of a broadcast or in a corner of the front page. They are the stories that people talk about around the coffee machine at work. They are the stories that cause a husband to call to his wife, "Hey Martha, come look at this!"

An aberration can take an ordinary story and transform it into the most talked-about item in the news.

3.3d What is Problem?

The most important stories usually involve a problem that needs to be solved. Our children can't read. Our water isn't fit to drink. Our streets aren't safe to drive. These are problems crying out for solutions, and thus they are news.

Sometimes the problem is revealed in a journalistic expose, such as Rachel Carson's "The Silent Spring." Sometimes they are revealed in the course of work-a-day reporting, such as The Washington Post's coverage of Watergate. Sometimes they spring upon us as a full-blown crisis, like the meltdown at Chernobyl.

The bigger the problem, the bigger the news.

But keep this in mind: To get a journalist's attention, the problem shouldn't have an immediate solution. If there is a solution at hand, then there is no news value. The problem is the story, not the solution.

Want an example? Take the U.S. space program. In the early 1960s, President Kennedy laid out a problem to be solved: Put a man on the moon by the end of the decade. The nation became consumed with solving the problem. Then, in 1969, the problem was solved. Neil Armstrong set foot on the moon. From that moment on, the space program had trouble keeping the attention of the news media and the American public.

The problem had been solved. It was no longer news.

3.3e How to Put Muscle on Your Story Proposal.

Let's say your company is opening a new widget plant. Immediately, you have change. But you should search for other elements within the story.

You find out that some industry experts think it's insane for a company to invest in a widget plant in the current economy. There's conflict.

You learn that your company's widget factory is the nation's first new widget factory since World War II. There's aberration.

You discover that your company must convince customers to embrace a revolutionary new design over cheap imports of an outdated, but functional design. There's your problem.

Now you've got a much stronger story to offer.

But be forewarned. Most companies will readily accept a story proposal that focuses on change and aberration. But most will resist proposals that point to conflicts and problems.

Stand your ground. If your job is to get your company into the news media, then it is your responsibility to insist that your company maximize its potential for news coverage. The trick is to do it in a way that does not harm or embarrass your company.

In this, you must be guided by common sense and good judgment. Look for conflicts and problems that portray your company as a hero or as an underdog. Do this, and resistance within your company will melt away.

Just as attorneys must keep their clients within the law, and accountants must keep their clients within generally accepted accounting principles, so must you—as your company's media relations counsel—prod your client or your boss to make the most of any opportunity to create news.

The PR Rainmaker knows: Change is news. But to really get attention, you must find a way to include conflict, aberration and problem in any story proposal.

3.4 Crisis: The Mother's Milk of the News Business

The news media love a crisis. Why? Because a crisis gives the media what they need most: Heroes, villains and very large audiences.

- The space shuttle blows up. The dead astronauts are heroes; the manufacturers and the designers of the O-rings are villains.

- Anthrax invades the U.S. Capitol. The investigators are the heroes, as are the brave staff members who stand up to the terror. The mysterious sender of the tainted letters is the villain.

- The nation goes to war. America's fighting soldiers as well as its national leaders are the heroes. The enemy is the villain: Kaiser Wilhelm, Adolf Hitler, General Tojo, Ho Chi Mihn, Saddam Hussein, Osama bin Laden.

The news media provide their highest value to the American people when they cover these genuine crises. As a result, it is during a crisis that the media attract their largest audiences. Newspapers sell out on the newsstands. TV ratings soar. (CNN's best ratings come during a crisis, such as the Gulf War, the Clinton impeachment or the September 11th attacks. It is between crises that CNN tends to lapse into low ratings, small audiences and inner turmoil.)

Thus, when there is no crisis, the news media will create one by taking a relatively small story and sensationalizing it. The list is long and familiar: apples 'poisoned' with insecticides, trade deficits with Japan, the disappearance of the family farm, a congressman's illicit sexual affair with a missing intern, and on and on.

These stories are designed to create heroes and villains in the public mind, and thus to attract large audiences. Indeed, the entire genre of the TV newsmagazine ("60 Minutes," "Dateline," "20/20") is based upon the need to create crises where they do not exist.

To make money, the news media must attract an audience. To attract an audience, the news media must create a crisis. And every crisis requires heroes and villains.

This is why your local TV station will race its camera crews to cover the burning of an abandoned warehouse, but will not devote five seconds to an upcoming bond election. The fire at least appears to be a crisis. It has a clear villain, the arsonist who set the fire. It has clear-cut heroes, the firefighters who battle the blaze.

Here's another example. A typical bond election is just another boring solution to a dull problem.

But this can change in a heartbeat if a gadfly group claims that the bond election is rigged by the city's powerful elite to divert taxpayer money into private pockets. At that point, the bond election becomes a scandal, and a scandal is a crisis. The news crews will then race to cover the bond election, not to explain its importance, but to amplify the crisis.

The PR Rainmaker understands this: Crisis is the mother's milk of American journalism.

All of this dates back to the late 1890s, when publisher Joseph Pulitzer created the genre of "crisis and response" to boost circulation of his New York World. His innovations—the front page, the headline, the news lead, the inverted pyramid story—still dominate journalism today in print, on the air and on the Internet.

Like most truly revolutionary ideas, Pulitzer's formula was starkly simple: Identify a crisis, gather responses, push for reform, praise the heroes, destroy the villains and ride the crusade until it runs out of momentum. Then repeat.

The formula remains intact a century later, covered only with a thin layer of self-righteousness and self-importance provided by the universities that train today's journalists.

You may be appalled at this formula. Clearly, this is not what the Founders had in mind when they wrote the First Amendment.

But PR Rainmakers accept the formula and put it to work in their favor.

3.5 The Secret Ingredient of News Coverage

Why do so many PR campaigns fall flat, failing to attract the media attention that their creators crave? For the same reason that a loaf of bread falls flat if you leave out the yeast. You've failed to add a small, but vital ingredient.

Like baking bread, creating news requires us to follow a recipe.

The secret but indispensable ingredient of that recipe—the ingredient that the flacks will ignore, overlook or avoid—is controversy.

Controversy is really nothing more than conflict combined with crisis. To understand why controversy is so vital to your success, you must understand the nature of news.

As presented in today's media, the news is not simply a rehashing of yesterday's events. When a reporter writes or broadcasts the news, what he is really doing is fabricating a story.

By "story," the PR Rainmaker means "an interesting tale filled with characters, action, plot and suspense."

Every major news story—whether it's the Gulf War, the Monica Lewinsky scandal, the World Trade Center attack or the Enron debacle—is an ongoing soap opera filled with larger-than-life characters, plot twists and high drama.

On a much small scale, the same is true about a local fire, a city council meeting or a school board election.

Think about it.

Take a house fire. It's the firefighters versus the consuming blaze, battling to save property and to preserve human life.

How about a city council meeting? It depends.

There are many things that occur at a council meeting that never appear in a news story. For example, few newspapers are likely to report that the council approved the minutes of the previous meeting. Why? Because there is no controversy.

But if the mayor is fighting with the council over whether to approve pay raises for the police department, that changes everything. Now you have a story. Now you have controversy.

This is the recipe for all news: big and small, hard or soft, national or local.

The raw materials of news are a change, a conflict, an aberration or a problem. These materials must then be presented as an on-going story that involves characters, action, plot and suspense.

But the catalyst—the secret ingredient that will transform your media campaign into major news coverage—is controversy. And lots of it.

If you want proof, pick up any daily newspaper in America. Study the articles you find there. You will find that every news item contains a story, just as certainly as will a Danielle Steel novel or a Steven Spielberg movie.

The news story will be told in the language of journalism: who, what, when, where, why and how. The writer will apply one of the standard structures of journalism, whether it's the Associated Press' inverted pyramid or the Wall Street Journal's feature formula.

But the article is still a story with heroes and villains, problems and solutions.

The story will also include a controversy. And the bigger the controversy, the bigger the news.

Indeed, without some kind of controversy, there is no real news. If a toddler falls down in her backyard, that's not news. But if that same toddler falls down an abandoned oil shaft, and the local emergency crews spend two days digging her out, now it's national news.

If four teenagers attend high school for the first time, that's not news. But if those four teenagers are the first African-Americans to attend a segregated high school in the Deep South, and the governor calls out the National Guard to stop them from entering the building, now that's national news.

That's the nature of news. And the PR Rainmaker knows how to take advantage of that nature.

Most PR specialists make sure they include the Five Ws and the H in every news release. Most are careful to portray their clients or companies in a favorable light. But you can accomplish all of this with advertising.

If you want publicity, if you want to attract a reporter's attention, then you must add controversy. And you must directly connect your company, its product or its service in some way to that controversy.

Now many intelligent, well-meaning executives will shudder at the idea of allowing their companies to be associated with a controversy. After all, doesn't a controversy mean "negative news?"

Not necessarily. The key is to position your company as the solution to the controversy, not as the cause. Do that, and your company becomes a hero while someone else or something else becomes the villain.

Basically, it's the difference between a mortar shell and a skyrocket. Both are made from explosives. But a mortar shell will destroy a building. A skyrocket will light up the night with beauty and wonder. It's all in how you package the ingredients.

The same holds true with controversy. Package it badly, and it will blow up in your face. Package it expertly, and you'll draw applause.

The PR Rainmaker knows: Controversy breeds coverage.

3.6 Pick Your Controversy with Care

As with any secret ingredient, controversy must be chosen wisely and carefully. Not just any controversy will do. You must pick a controversy that will serve you well.

To ignite a controversy, you must first point out a threat to the public. Second, you must identify the villain responsible for that threat. Third, you must position your company as the hero that opposes the threat and the villain.

All of this must be done subtly. The public must never see your company pulling the strings. If you appear to be setting up a straw man just to knock it down, you will lose credibility rather than gain it.

Let's begin with the task of finding, isolating and identifying a risk to the public. The place to start is with your product or service. What problem does it solve? Whom does it serve?

All business is a matter of solving a problem for someone. A plumber solves the problems of leaking faucets and back-up sewers. A tax attorney solves the problems of IRS audits and unsheltered income. A convenience store solves the problem of needing the quick purchase of a quart of milk.

Every company solves at least one problem. Spend some time analyzing the problems your company solves every day. Make a list. Go over the list with your employees or co-workers. Uncover every problem or potential problem that your company can handle.

Beside each listed problem, list the categories of customers or clients that would use your service to solve these problems. Include not only current categories, but also categories you believe you should be reaching, but aren't.

Don't worry about going overboard. Later on, you can always scratch out any categories that don't make sense.

For now, just brainstorm.

3.6a Ask Three Questions to Find a Threat

The next step is to weigh each of these identified problems as a true threat to the public. We do this by asking ourselves three questions about each problem:

- Is this a problem that will truly create an intense concern among our consumers?

- Is the probability high—or, at least, moderate—that the average consumer will face this problem at some time?

- Is your company clearly an expert in studying, confronting or solving this problem?

If the answer is yes to all three questions, you have a solid candidate for a threat that you can tackle in the news media.

3.6b Choose a Threat with No Immediate Solution

To work as a news story, the threat must be something that will worry the average reader or viewer. To work as a news source, you or your company must present itself as an expert about the problem.

Here's a very important point to remember about the "expert" factor: It's not necessary for you to have an immediate solution to the problem. In fact, it's usually better that the threat not have an immediate solution.

Here's a recent example: the "energy crisis" from the summer of 2001. For weeks, the national news was dominated by soaring prices at the gas pump and by rolling electrical blackouts along the West Coast. Judging from the intensity of the coverage, one might have thought civilization was about to end. Behind the scenes, the federal government took action to increase the supplies of both gasoline and electricity.

Prices fell. Blackouts ended.

Suddenly, the story was no longer a story.

Is the problem gone? Of course not. The United States remains a slave to Saudi oil. But the immediate threat was solved, and the news value was destroyed.

The threat remains news only as long as it remains a threat. A solution resolves the on-going news story, and thus kills its news value.

However, as an expert, it is good for you to propose a solution that is:

- Innovative. You identify a problem, then propose a solution that other experts are missing.

- In the works. You identify a problem, then propose a solution that is plausible, but that will require commitment from someone important—the public, the government, the private sector, etc.—to develop and produce. If you can demonstrate that your company is taking the lead in discovering this solution, that's even better.

The PR Rainmaker knows: When you choose a controversy, make sure it's one with a long shelf life.

3.7 News is a Doughnut

One of the saddest ordeals you will ever suffer through in PR is to watch a perfectly good story go stale, due to corporate bureaucracy.

The process usually starts well enough. Something newsworthy happens within the company. Everyone recognizes it and agrees that a reporter should be informed.

The PR department quickly knocks out a press release. The CEO gives the release an initial blessing.

And then bureaucracy takes over.

The marketing department wants to see a copy. So does the legal department. Then someone shoots a faxed copy over to the new client, and its CEO, and its marketing department, and its legal team all take a look at it.

By now, the release no longer resembles the original draft. Your PR team does its best to reshape the release, then sends it to the CEO, who again blesses the draft.

If you're lucky, you can now send out the release.

There's just one problem. Weeks have passed. Your news is no longer news. It's history.

Journalists are in the news business. Your story has lost its timeliness, and with it you've lost all those news media that would have been interested in your story when it was fresh.

There's nothing at all rare about this scenario. It happens every day in companies across the nation and around the world.

CEOs and marketers and lawyers do not understand the difference between news and history. Don't expect them to know what you know. As a PR Rainmaker, it is your job to recognize the difference and act accordingly.

So how do you prevent your story from going stale? You do it with a combination of organization, persistence and fanaticism.

Your PR machine should be every bit as well-designed and well-maintained as any manufacturing plant:

- Install a formal system for generating PR.

- Set specific procedures and schedules for issuing all releases.

- Establish who will see the story and in what order.

- Give each department a set amount of time to approve the release. Insist that deadlines be met.

- Make it clear that the job is not to rewrite the release, but only to correct errors.

Push, push, push until you have a finished release. Then get that release out with the next news cycle. Put it in the hands of those who can turn your release into news.

Time is of the essence in PR. You do your company a major disservice if you fail to ramrod your release through the system just as quickly as you can.

The PR Rainmaker knows: News is like a doughnut. You either serve it fresh or you don't serve it at all.

3.8 Sell Your Company Through Credibility

Few in the business world understand the primary goal of a public relations campaign. They confuse its goal with that of marketing and advertising. This results in a mish-mash of strategies and tactics that waste much money while producing few results.

The primary job of marketing is to attract consumers. The primary job of PR is to create a public climate that will allow marketing to do its job effectively.

PR Rainmaking sets the stage for effective marketing by creating credibility for your company, your product or your service.

Yet most executives view PR in the narrow context of the press agent. They want to "generate clips." They want "good press." They want "our name in the papers."

If this is all you want, then hire a good secretary. All it takes to get your "name in the papers" is a set of passable writing skills, some letterhead and some envelopes, postage stamps and a telephone. Throw in a fax machine and an e-mail provider, and you have everything you need to "generate clips."

Of course, it is unlikely those clips will actually help you to attract customers and clients.

Why? Because those clips will provide little or no information on who you are, what you do and why anyone would want to use your product or service.

They will do nothing to power your marketing efforts.

On the upside, you will have a very nice scrapbook to share with friends and family.

Unfortunately, the broad spectrum of PR agencies do nothing to dispel the notion of the PR specialist as little more than an press agency. Most agencies are more than happy to accept the client's instructions to "get out there and get us in the media."

These agencies write press releases that are designed to gratify the CEO's ego rather than actually attract media coverage.

They create media kits that are beautiful to behold, but impossible for a reporter to use.

They invest thousands of dollars in video news releases that litter the floors of TV stations across the nation.

They use the "spray and pray" method of distribution, sending out faxes and emails to a long list of reporters who will not use their news items.

Indeed, PR is the 21st century has been largely reduced to the equivalent of junk mail and telemarketing.

It's a damn shame.

3.8a Bernays' Grand Vision of PR

When Edward L. Bernays invented the concept of "public relations" during the early 20th century, his aspirations reached much higher than one could guess by watching the profession practiced today.

Here is how Bernays, in an interview with author Stuart Ewen, defined the public relations professional:

> *"An applied social scientist who advises a client or employer on the social attitudes and actions to take to win the support of the publics upon whom his or her or its vitality depends."*

According to Bernays, a PR counsel keeps a careful eye on the public, watching for the trends that might affect his client's future.

More than that, the PR counsel advises his client on how to put these trends to an advantage, or even how to change opinions and behaviors in ways that will benefit the client.

Bernays considered PR advice to be far more valuable to a company's future than legal advice "because legal advice is based on precedent but public relations advice might actually establish precedent."

Somewhere along the way, the PR profession of Bernays' vision became the PR industry of today, bent more upon manufacturing "deliverables" than upon engineering consent.

No wonder laymen are powerless to even define PR. They are unable to distinguish PR from marketing or advertising because today's PR specialists fail to make the distinction themselves.

No wonder journalists dismiss today's PR specialists as flacks: brainless, aimless and immoral.

3.8b Credibility Leads to Profitability

For the PR Rainmaker, the first and foremost goal is always to create credibility.

Our immediate task may be to establish the credibility of a particular product, service, movement, idea or company. The task may be to create credibility with customers, prospects, employees, venders, investors or the general public.

But the first goal must always be credibility, and nothing else.

Why credibility?

Because credibility shapes public opinion.

Because credibility changes public behavior.

Because credibility sets the stage for the ready acceptance of any messages we may want to transmit through advertising or other marketing methods.

Because without credibility, no company, organization, professional or entrepreneur can hope to survive—much less thrive—in today's business environment.

The PR Rainmaker keeps this goal firmly in mind at all times, no matter what the situation, no matter what strategy:

Establish credibility and success will follow.

And what is the fastest way to establish credibility with both the public and the media?

By creating news—and lots of it.

3.9 Build Every Campaign Around a Targeted Newsworthy Appeal

All of the PR Rainmaker's rules, techniques and observations comes together in one concept: the Targeted Newsworthy Appeal.

Every story proposal, every media document, every PR campaign should be built around a simple TNA that can be expressed in a minimum of words.

The TNA becomes the North Star for the PR Rainmaker's efforts. It keeps the work on track and prevents the campaign from becoming diffuse and ineffective.

It is the practical and pragmatic tool that separates the PR professional from the mere flack.

The three parts of the TNA are:

- Targeted. We know our audiences specifically. We know their current behaviors. We know how we want their behaviors to change. We know whose opinion they respect and heed. We know which leaders they follow. We know which news media will reach them.

- Newsworthy. We understand what makes a story newsworthy. We look to combine change, conflict, aberration and problem into an attractive package. We embrace controversy as a tool for sparking the news media to pay attention. We move quickly to avoid spoiling the timeliness of our story.

- Appeal. We study the systems and habits of the news media we want to target, and exploit them to our benefit. We commit overt acts that attract attention. We make it easy for the reporter to cover our story the way we want it covered. We meet the reporter's deadlines. We combine all of these considerations to create an appeal that the news media cannot resist.

Building the TNA is not an option for the PR Rainmaker. It is an absolute necessity.

Without a Targeted Newsworthy Appeal, we waste time, money and effort that no company can afford to squander.

PR Rainmaking in Action, Part One:
How to Create News With an 'Overt Act'

4.1 To Make News, Commit an Overt Act

"An overt act is often necessary before an event can be regarded as news," said the Father of PR, Edward L. Bernays.

Bernays understated the case.

News requires an action.

Without an action, it becomes impossible to create news value and newsworthiness. Few reporters will recognize news without an action to report.

Legendary journalist Walter Lippmann, in his 1929 classic *Public Opinion*, explains this phenomenon by offering the example of a hypothetical banker named John Smith who declares bankruptcy.

It is the filing of the bankruptcy that reveals the news about Smith's situation, Lippmann says. His friends may have known about his problems. Rumors may have swirled. But until Smith took the overt act of filing for bankruptcy, there was little chance of Smith's finances becomes newsworthy.

"There is in these rumors nothing definite on which to peg the story," Lippmann says. (Remember: The "peg" is what provides the story with its timeliness. It is the event that gives the journalist an excuse to write about the subject.)

"Something definite must occur that has unmistakable form," Lippmann says. "It may be the act of going into bankruptcy, it may be a fire, a collision, an assault, a riot, an arrest, a denunciation, an introduction of a bill, a speech, a vote, a meeting, the expressed opinion of well-known citizen, an editorial in a newspaper, a sale, a wage-schedule, a price change, the proposal to build a bridge...There must be a manifestation. The course of events must assume a certain definable shape, and until it is in a phase where some aspect is an accomplished fact, news does not separate itself from the ocean of possible truth."

This is why journalists tend to hang around certain buildings, such as courthouses and city halls, and to attend certain events, such as criminal trials and public meetings. They are looking for overt acts that will signal a newsworthy story.

Therefore, the PR Rainmaker knows: If you seek to create news, you must commit an overt act.

4.2 Seven Ways to Act Overtly

There are at least seven overt acts that the news media eagerly cover over and over again. You will find these acts scattered throughout every news cycle if you watch for them.

Why?

As with any industry, the news media tend to fall into predictable patterns. When you're moving as quickly as reporters, editors and producers do, you are bound to fall into trends and habits. Much of what the media report is the result of conditioned response rather than careful thought.

The PR Rainmaker knows how to take advantage of these reactions to create predictable opportunities—overt acts—that will generate publicity. These methods work across the board. They work in local markets as well as on the national scene. They work for print as well as broadcast.

None of them is easy. Each requires much creative though and careful planning. Never attempt to execute one of these methods in a half-ass manner.

They are:

a.   Be first in a category.

b.   Forecast the future.

c.   Throw a brick.

d.   Release a survey.

e.   Issue a study.

f.   Offer a celebrity.

g.   Pull a stunt.

4.2a Be First in A Category

Who was the first pilot to complete a solo flight across the Atlantic from New York to Paris? The answer is Charles Lindbergh.

The 1927 feat rocketed Lindbergh from obscurity to lifelong fame. Newspapers followed his every move for years after his historic flight. History continues to rank his name among the most famous Americans ever.

Who was the second pilot to complete a solo flight across the Atlantic from New York to Paris?

The correct answer is: Who cares?

Such is the difference between being first and being second.

The PR Rainmaker knows: To make a splash in the news media, it always helps to be the first to accomplish something significant.

Do you have to do something as earth-shattering as Lindbergh did to get attention? Not at all.

But what you do first needs to be significant to someone somewhere.

The significance might be within your geographic area: Your company is the first in your state to open trade relations with Cuba.

The significance might be within your industry: Your company is the first in its industry to adopt a cutting-edge software.

The significance might be political: Your company is the first to publicly support legislation that will cut back on air pollution from utility plants.

The key is to be first in a well-defined category.

If the significance is geographical, take your story to your local newspapers. If the significance is industrial, take your story to the trade publications. If the significance is political, take it to both the mainstream media and the trade media.

The method of arriving at a "first" is: Focus, focus, focus.

Let's say that your company has signed an agreement to export bottled beer to China. If you are the first in the nation, you've got a chance at a national business story in The Wall Street Journal or Business Week.

But let's say you are the second company to sign such a contract. You're out of luck. Or are you?

For example, say a rival company is already exporting a national brand to China, but your company is the first to export a microbrew. Or a light beer. Or a near-bear. Now you've got a "first." You might still get that national story.

Now let's say that your company is well behind the curve nationally. Twenty other companies have beat you to the Chinese market and they've covered every category from premium beer to ice brew.

You may be out of the running for a national story, but if you're the first company in Georgia to export beer to China, then you can probably interest the Atlanta Journal-Constitution. If you're the first in Chicago, you can probably interest the business section of the Chicago Tribune.

Have you noticed? You have created a TNA, a Targeted Newsworthy Appeal.

Your story is now targeted to an industry or a location; it is now newsworthy because it is significant and timely; and it appeals to a deeply ingrained media tendency to report a "first."

The PR Rainmaker knows: The media love "firsts." And often all it takes to create a "first" is to gradually narrow the category until a "first" pops into view.

4.2b Forecast the Future

Why are the weather report, the horoscope and the Las Vegas betting lines among the most popular items in any daily newspaper? Because people love to be told what the future holds.

We Americans tend to live more in the future than in the present. We are always contemplating what we are going to do and seldom contemplate what we are doing in the moment.

This is why Zen Buddhism is so difficult for the average Westerner. It requires one to live in this moment, right now.

We'd rather be thinking about where we're going to eat lunch, what we're going to say at that important sales meeting, how much fun we're going to have during next week's vacation in Aspen.

The PR Rainmaker uses this tendency to an advantage. If you want to make news, make a bold prediction about what the future has in store for a targeted audience.

Companies large and small create headlines every week by making bold predictions based upon their in-house research.

Take these examples that made news during the last two weeks of May 2002:

- The home fragrance market will top $3.4 billion by 2006, an increase of 24 percent, according to the Web site MarketResearch.com

- World Markets Research Centre said the five-year growth patterns of third generation mobile telecommunication companies will fall below expectations. WMRC is a risk analysis company in England.

- The number of outsourced business e-mailboxes will double to almost 119 million by 2006, according to The Radicati Group Inc., a consulting firm in Palo Alto, Calif.

- U.S. public schools will increase their spending on information technology to $9.5 billion by the 2005–2006 school year, says the online learning program at IDC, a technology advisor in Framingham, Mass.

- Digital TV will reach into 73 percent of European homes by 2008, according to London-based research company Strategy Analytics.

You will note some similarities among these predictions.

First, to make news, a prediction must be bold. You have to stick out your neck a bit and be willing to be wrong. You can say things are going to be better than expected, or worse. The point is: It's the bold who make news. If you forecast is both bold and contrarian, so much the better.

Second, a prediction must be based upon an interpretation of facts and trends. To have credibility, you must back your claim with data and logic.

Third, your prediction must matter to someone other than yourself. It must appeal to a readily identifiable audience of some significant size.

In short: Search your data for trends, make a courageous forecast based upon those trends and offer it to a media outlet with an audience that cares.

When you do these things well, you build a Targeted Newsworthy Appeal that will land positive media coverage for you and your company.

The PR Rainmaker knows: Make a bold but logical prediction about a meaningful issue, and you will make news.

4.2c Throw a Brick

Walter Winchell was the most influential newspaper columnist of the 1930s and 1940s, a time when newspapers were the most powerful media in the world. He rose from obscurity as a third-rate vaudeville performer to become feared, hated and widely imitated.

His formula for success?

"The fastest way to become famous," he said, "is to throw a brick at someone famous."

Winchell fought publicly with entertainment's biggest names, from Al Jolson to Josephine Baker to Lucille Ball. Later in his career, he swung toward political reporting. Winchell championed an unprecedented third term for President Franklin Roosevelt as well as the Red Scare for Joe McCarthy.

He threw bricks in every direction. And this made him among the most famous men in the nation.

Winchell's tactics have been adopted and adapted by scores of ambitious individuals and organizations.

How did Ralph Nader become famous? By attacking General Motors.

How did Jesse Jackson become famous? By claiming that racism is systemic at virtually every major U.S. corporation, then attacking those corporations one by one: Anheuser-Busch, AT&T, Viacom, Verizon, Ford and on and on. Not only has this made him famous, it has made him wealthy, with an annual income estimated to exceed $300,000.

How did style guru Mr. Blackwell become famous? By issuing an annual list of the Worst Dressed Women in the World, and thus attacking some of the most famous females on the planet. After more than four decades, Mr. Blackwell's list remains among the most anticipated—and dreaded—bricks in all of entertainment and fashion. Among his recent victims: Princess Stephanie, pop singer Britney Spears, game show host Anne Robinson, royal companion Camilla Parker Bowles, film star Kate Hudson and TV actress Gillian Anderson.

The same basic tactic is repeated everywhere you look: in politics, in government and in business. Throw the right brick at the right person, and you gain fame.

Obviously, throwing a brick isn't for everyone. It takes a strong stomach, a steady nerve and the willingness to dodge a few bricks thrown in your direction.

But it works.

The keys to creating a Targeted Newsworthy Appeal with this tactic are to find the right brick and the right target.

The right brick is a criticism or a charge that:

- Your target cannot easily deny or dismiss with a few well-chosen words.

- Arouses your target audience—your potential customers or clients—to take action against the target.

- Brings your issue into stark clarity for the public to see, to study and to digest.

The right target is:

- An industry leader with a well-known brand name.

- A famous person who practices or champions what you oppose.

The PR Rainmaker knows: Winchell was right. If you want to become famous fast, throw a brick.

4.2d Release a Survey

Americans care what others think. We have little choice.

We live in a representative democracy. Our plans and goals may be thwarted by how the others around us act and vote. We need to know not only how they think, but what we can say that might persuade them to think our way instead.

As a result, we are obsessed with opinion polls. Look through any major newspaper in the United States, and you will find survey after survey on what people are thinking about today.

The media's appetite for such surveys is virtually insatiable. Surveys not only sway voters, consumers, politicians and executives, they also entertain readers in a very specific way.

The all-time corporate champ of the publicity survey has to be the Gallup Organization. So frequent are the company's appearances in the media that the word "Gallup" is virtually synonymous with "poll."

Would it surprise you to learn that Gallup is not primarily a public opinion company, but rather a business-consulting firm? And yet Gallup has become a household word with its inspired choices for polling data.

One recent Gallup survey showed that a majority of doctors were not instructing their patients on the proper use of blood pressure medications. Another showed that 70 percent of U.S. expectant mothers were not taking Vitamin B, though they clearly understood the supplement would help prevent birth defects.

Now each of those is a real news story. One shows that doctors are failing in their duties, while another shows that mothers are failing in theirs. The surveys provided crucial, yet astounding, data for the news media to use as launching boards for their own stories.

The PR Rainmaker knows: If you want to learn how to create studies that get media attention, study Gallup.

Apparently, many organizations are already are taking that advice. Consider these recent examples:

- The National School Boards Foundation discovered that the students—and not the teachers—are the campus experts in school technology at more than half of the nation's school districts. The poll surveyed 811 school districts, including 90 of the 100 largest.

- Author Alan Cohen supported the release of his new book, "Why Your Life Sucks," by hiring the Harris Poll to find out why most Americans find their lives disappointing. The poll found that most Americans—25 percent—blame their boss. Harris sampled 2,500 respondents for the poll.

- Drug manufacturer GlaxoSmithKline released a four-city survey that showed that only 26 percent of men who are tested for sexually transmitted diseases are testing for genital herpes. The survey, conducted by RoperASW, talked to 800 subjects in New York City, Chicago, Atlanta and San Diego. GlaxoSmithKline is the maker of VALTREX, a prescription suppressant for genital herpes.

To create a Targeted Newsworthy Appeal, a survey must provide a result that is controversial, if not sensational:

- Students know more about technology than do their teachers.

- Americans blame their bosses for their personal disappointments.

- Sexually active men are failing to test for genital herpes.

In addition, a survey with media appeal should be conducted in a scientific manner and by a credible third party.

In other words, don't execute the survey yourself. Spend the extra bucks and hire a professional to do it right. Short cuts will yield disappointing results.

4.2e Issue a Study

Using a study to attract media attention is the second cousin to using a survey.

To successfully create a Targeted Newsworthy Appeal, the study should confirm or deny some controversial and newsworthy issue.

For example:

- Forty-five percent of the world's top 250 companies included reports on corporate responsibility in their 2002 disclosure statements, according to professional services firm KPMG. That's up from 35 percent in 1999, reflecting a trend toward higher accountability to shareholders, KPMG said.

- The siblings of people who live past age 100 also tend to live much longer than the average human, according to a June 2002 study sponsored by biogen firm Centagenetix. (Fittingly enough, Centagenetix works with the connection between genetics and longevity. Thus, the study helped to elevate the small company's credibility in the public eye.)

Unlike the survey, it is permissible to pull the study from your company's own vault of research.

The consulting firm PricewaterhouseCoopers (for example) releases a national quarterly study of venture capital transactions. PWC breaks the data down by region, industry, source and size. By providing this invaluable data to the VC sector, PWC positions itself as the expert consultant in the field.

In most cases, however, it is better to have a qualified third party certify your results to add credibility.

Like its cousin the survey, the study creates a Targeted Newsworthy Appeal by providing an interesting, controversial or sensational answer to a question with broad appeal. The study is particularly useful for piggybacking on a national or international news story, such as the Sept. 11 terrorist attacks.

Any company can build a powerful reputation with this one tactic: issuing newsworthy study after newsworthy study.

If you want to learn how, pay particular attention to the studies issued by high-profile consultants like PricewaterhouseCoopers and KPMG, or by well-known activist groups like Common Cause or Public Citizen. They know how to execute the study-as-publicity-tool better than anyone.

4.2f Offer a Celebrity

There are few better ways to get attention from almost any news medium than to bring in a celebrity to spread your message.

It almost doesn't matter how tenuous the connection between the celebrity and your issue. Remember when activist groups brought out actress Sissy Spacek to address a Congressional committee on the plight of the family farm? Now Sissy Spacek is a wonderful actress, but her connection to the "family farm" issue is that she once played a farm wife in a movie. Still, her testimony attracted serious news coverage from the TV networks and the national newspapers.

Why? Because she was a famous face talking about a hot topic.

Still, it does help to have a strong connection between the celebrity and your issue if you want your message to resonate in the public mind.

Take, for example, a company in Los Angeles known as Spotlight Health, which specializes in producing health awareness campaigns that feature celebrities.

In June 2002, Spotlight Health brought together rock singer Ian Anderson of Jethro Tull, former Vice President Dan Quayle and Olympic skater Tara Lipinski to draw attention to deep vein thrombosis. DVP affects more than 2 million Americans and kills 200,000 annually, more than the combined annual total of breast cancer, AIDS and highway accidents.

The connection? Anderson, Quayle and Lipinski all suffer from DVP.

Spotlight Health has a strong track record of attracting media attention to health issues through celebrities. The company has brought in talk show host Larry King to discuss heart disease, singer Carnie Wilson to talk about morbid obesity, plus sportscaster Bob Uecker and former Sen. Bob Dole to put the spotlight on abdominal aortic aneurysms.

Spotlight Health knows that the news media love to cover a familiar face discussing a vital issue of the day. Why? Because readers, viewers and listeners love it.

The media are in business to attract an audience. Almost nothing keeps an audience in place better than a celebrity talking about something important.

For example, Olympic speed skater Erik Henriksen led an in-line skating team called the MSN Butterfly Bladers into downtown Chicago in June 2002. Their mission? To demonstrate to the media how Chicagoans can fill their "slow time" by using the Web-enabled Verizon Wireless phone to send email, track stocks, check the weather and get news.

If the celebrity is big enough, then just showing up is enough to bring out the media.

When Wal-Mart wanted publicity in a small market back during the 1990s, it would send its billionaire founder Sam Walton to the store to shake hands with his customers. That almost always brought out the news cameras.

Today, if Microsoft wants to assure publicity, to trots out Bill Gates. If McDonald's wants news coverage, it sends Ronald McDonald. If Wheaties wants media attention, it bring in the latest "hot athlete" who will soon appear on the cereal's box covers.

The technique can also be subtle.

Launching a new cooking utensil? Send out a famous chef to make the rounds of TV morning shows to demonstrate how your product can improve home cooking.

Selling a line of cosmetics? Hire a well-known face to serve as a fashion expert who recommends your product through soft news items in print and on TV.

You can even combine the celebrity tactic with other tactics to enhance your Targeted Newsworthy Appeal. A celebrity can speak at a news conference that issues your survey or study. A celebrity can participate in a publicity stunt. A celebrity can throw a brick.

The PR Rainmaker knows: Give a celebrity something to do in public, and the news media will come running.

4.2g Pull a Stunt

There are PR professionals who will tell you the stunt is dead, that it went out with P.T Barnum.

Bunk.

Anyone with eyes, ears and a brain can recognize that the stunt is alive and well. Indeed, there is virtually no better way to attract TV coverage than with a well-planned, highly visual stunt.

TV producers love great pictures. If the picture is hot enough, the producer will find some excuse to pass off the picture as news.

With the vast majority of Americans getting their news from television, the PR Rainmaker knows that great pictures translate into a wide dispersal of a well-honed image.

Activists know this. That's why they chain themselves to old growth trees and why they wear outlandish costumes to upstage politicians they oppose. Can anyone remember the purpose of "Hands Across America" back in the 1990s? Can anyone forget the image of thousands of Americans holding hands along city streets, across bridges and down highways?

Corporate America knows the power of the visual stunt as well.

Among the best occurred in March 2001 as the news media was transfixed on the pending re-entry of Mir, a 150-ton space station. Around the world, experts bickered over exactly where the space station would crash and how much havoc it would cause.

Amid all of this, Taco Bell placed a 40-foot by 40-foot floating target in the South Pacific Ocean, off the coast of Australia. The restaurant chain announced to the world that, if any part of the Mir station hit the target, every American would receive a free taco.

The stunt received almost as much coverage as the Mir station itself. TV stations across the globe fed their viewers images of the massive Taco Bell target floating in the choppy waters.

Why? First, it was funny. But more importantly, the stunt finally gave TV producers something to show other than computer simulations of the Mir's flight path.

The picture was manna from heaven for these TV producers. And Taco Bell, for a few thousand dollars, reaped several million dollars in airtime.

The execution was perfect: Taco Bell piggybacked on an international event with a strong visual element, did it with humor and did it on the cheap.

But there's another lesson here: Taco Bell took a risk.

First, there was a real chance that a piece of Mir would hit the target and Taco Bell would be forced to pay up. As it turned out, the Russian station landed thousands of miles away. But the risk was there.

However, it was a positive risk. Even if Taco Bell had lost the bet, thousands of Americans who had never tried Taco Bell would have sampled the company's product. That's not a terrible gamble to take.

The other major risk was that, as some experts predicted, Mir would have crashed into a populated area, killed hundreds and made Taco Bell look like an insensitive lout.

Here, Taco Bell took a calculated risk. Two-thirds of the planet is ocean. The odds were clearly on Taco Bell's side.

But if you're going to pull a stunt, you must always understand and careful gauge the risk involved. A stunt can turn sour. That's why careful planning is essential.

Later, we will discuss a very special form of stunt known as "brandstanding."

For now, suffice it to say: A great stunt is your ticket to wide news coverage. However, it takes an equal amount of brains and guts to pull off a successful stunt.

PR Rainmaking in Action, Part Two: How to Create News With a 'Trojan Horse'

5.1 Getting Past the Gates

The Ancient Greeks wasted almost 20 years trying to scale the walls of Troy. They launched one assault after another, losing scores of their best warriors in each attempt. Finally, the Greek generals settled upon an audacious plan.

They built a gigantic and beautiful horse made of wood. They left this gift outside the Trojan gates, then sailed away.

The victorious Trojans dragged the massive statue through their gates. They celebrated all day and into the night. Finally, the exhausted Trojans fell asleep. What they didn't know was that the Greeks had hidden a team of crack troops inside the horse.

Early the next morning, these soldiers slipped out of the horse and opened the city gates wide. In poured the Greek army, which had quietly returned to the shores of Troy while the city had celebrated its victory.

Within minutes, the 20-year struggle was over. The Greek had won their war by giving the Trojans what they wanted most: a symbol of victory.

In the world of public relations, the PR specialists are the Greeks and the news media are the Trojans.

PR specialists launch one assault after another, using a barrage of press releases, phone calls, media kits, gift packages and other weapons with the hope that the Trojans will open their gates.

The news media, on the other hand, fight desperately to keep out the PR messages they consider dull, self-serving or irrelevant.

The war goes on day after day, week after week, year after year.

It is the major reason why journalists hold PR "flacks" in such contempt.

The PR Rainmakers understands: If you want to get inside the gates of Troy, you must build a Trojan Horse.

You must create a news package that the news media will find attractive and will drag inside their gates. Hidden inside that package are your key messages, waiting to jump out and take control.

Here's what it takes to build a Trojan Horse the media will find tough to resist.

There are five basic parts:

   a.   Crisis/solution.

   b.   Hero/villain.

   c.   Supporting data.

   d.   Third-party comments.

   e.   Visuals.

5.1a Crisis/Solution

As we've discussed, the lifeblood of the news media is crisis. It's your job to come up with a crisis that your company can solve. It's not that difficult.

Whatever product or service your company offers, it solves a problem for somebody.

Accountants solve tax problems. Plumbers solve water and waste problems. Cars solve transportation problems.

Ask yourself seriously: What problems does my company solve? How could those problems create a crisis for our customers?

5.1b Hero/Villain

The hero is obvious. It's your company.

Every hero needs a villain. In this case, the villain is whoever or whatever is causing the problem that is threatening to become a crisis.

You must identify that villain carefully and clearly.

If you make a software that cures computer viruses, then the villains are the hackers who create those viruses. If you exterminate houses, then the villains are the bugs and vermin that bring in the germs that can make a family ill.

Without a villain, your Trojan Horse is incomplete.

5.1c Supporting Data

Comb through the research your company and your industry have produced. Use official numbers and statistics to demonstrate the scope of the crisis.

The emotion causes the media to buy into your story; the data provides the logic that closes the sales.

Don't get cute with the numbers.

Find a solid source and let the numbers talk for themselves.

5.1d Third-party Experts

Supply a long list of experts who can comment on your crisis.

These experts can come from colleges, think tanks, industry groups or consulting firms. But they must have nothing to do with you or your company.

You must provide experts for the news media to use to verify your story. Don't worry too much whether the experts agree with you point for point.

As long as they buy into your crisis and they have nothing to do with your company, they will suffice.

It doesn't hurt to toss in a few experts who completely disagree with your ideas. Third-party experts are there to enhance your credibility with the news media.

By providing these experts, you solve a major problem for any reporter you deal with.

5.1e Visuals

Most news media are visual. Newspapers use photos, graphics and charts. Television uses taped footage and live shots.

If you want to make your story attractive to the media, you must provide visuals. You must give the media a choice. You will offer a package of photos, footage and other visuals. Or you will provide the news media with the chance to shoot their own photos and footage.

Some media will jump at the chance to save time and money by using your finished product. Most prefer to send their own photographers or to use their own graphic artists. You must be ready for either situation.

5.2 The Trojan Horse at Work

So how does this work in a real-life situation? How do you build a Trojan Horse with a Targeted Newsworthy Appeal?

Let's say you are working for an air-conditioning company that wants to get its latest machine onto TV news programs. The unit is the most energy-efficient machine the company has ever built.

First, what is the crisis? Air-conditioners cool off homes during the summer. But they can be expensive to run during the hottest months, especially if a home lacks proper insulation. You study the newspapers and you learn that energy costs are expected to rise this year. So the crisis becomes: Home owners will pay high energy prices this summer if they fail to prepare.

What is the solution? Use proper insulation and other cool-saving technique to get your home ready for summer. And consider replacing your inefficient, outdated AC unit with a modern, highly efficient machine that will pay for itself in the long run.

Second, who is the villain? It's the trio of high energy costs, poor insulation and inefficient AC units.

Third, where is the supporting data? The federal government offers numbers that demonstrate an energy-efficient home can lower the costs of home cooling significantly. Just installing storm doors and windows can cut cooling costs by 30 percent, according to Uncle Sam. That is the sort of convincing data you want to collect and to package for the media to use.

Fourth, who are the third-party experts? If you had wanted print coverage, you would want to compile a long list of experts from industry, government and universities to comment on the need for energy efficiency. But since you are aiming just for television, you can create your own third-party expert by using a company spokesman. This spokesman must understand clearly that his role is to deliver the crisis/solution script, not to hawk a commercial message. You want your spokesman to come across as a Bob Villa or a Martha Stewart. As long as the spokesman sticks to information and stays away from commercialism, he will be accepted as a third-party expert.

Fifth, what are the visuals? When dealing with television, you must be prepared to offer one of four scenarios. One is to provide your own footage with what is known as B-roll. This is the footage that the station broadcasts while the anchor or the reporter provides voice-over. Another is for the station to send a camera crew to your location to shoot their own footage. A third is for your spokesman to take part in a live, in-studio interview. The fourth is for the camera crew to come to your site for a live, on-location segment. You never know which of these the TV producer will want. As a result, you must be ready for all four. The imperative in any of these scenarios is movement. TV demands that things move. Think it through. What can we show? How can we show it? What do we have on hand that moves?

The example of the air-conditioning client is a real one. There are few products on earth less interesting to watch than an air-conditioning unit. They have a bad habit of just sitting there.

So we created a TV package we called "Summer-ize Your Home."

We coached a company spokesman on energy-saving tips, such as insulation, storm windows, landscaping and such. This positioned him as the hero out to fight the villain, which was high energy costs.

For B-roll, we took the spokesman to a construction site where we shot interviews with him talking about these tips. We then shot footage of an actor demonstrating these tips: rolling out insulation, installing a storm door, and so on. Among these tips was the need to maintain your air-conditioning unit and to consider replacing an outdated unit with a new one. The B-roll allowed us to include footage of the product as an actor pretended to clean, service and install the company's new product. We then delivered the B-roll along with a suggested script.

One station used the script without a single change, as well as the B-roll footage. Others liked the overall idea, but wanted to add their own spin.

One wanted an in-studio interview with the spokesman. So we built several props that allowed the spokesman to demonstrate the tips as he described them. We also delivered a large AC unit for the spokesman to handle while he discussed the importance of new AC technology.

Another station wanted to shoot its own footage, so we returned to the construction site and went through the production a second time.

A fourth station wanted a live, on-location interview for its morning news program. So we invited the crew to a finished home, where the spokesman took the reporter on a live tour of an energy-efficient house.

Timing was everything on this project. The TV producers had to feel the crisis was at hand. We provided copies of news stories that backed our claims that energy costs were about to boom. But it wasn't until local thermometers began to top 90 degrees F. that the stations clamored for our package. We landed 17 hits over an eight-week period.

"Summer-ize Your Home" was a classic Trojan Horse. We built a package around a Targeted Newsworthy Appeal that we knew the TV stations would find attractive. We then waited for the gatekeepers to drag our package inside the station. Once we were inside, our messages could leap out and make themselves known.

The PR Rainmaker knows: Why storm the walls when you can win a decisive victory with a carefully conceived, well-constructed Trojan Horse?

PR Rainmaking in Action, Part Three: How to Create News With a 'Brandstanding' Event

6.1 Transform a Stunt into a Brandstand

There are many ways to get attention with a publicity stunt. Most risk making you look cheap or silly. The best method is to produce a stunt that doesn't look like a stunt. This is the "brandstanding" event.

Brandstanding is just what it sounds like. It is grandstanding in support of your brand. You are creating an event to get publicity. Not a stunt, but an event.

The PR Rainmaker knows that, when properly executed, the brandstanding event accomplishes three objectives at one time.

- First, it creates close contact between your brand and your customers.

- Second, it attracts TV and newspaper cameras.

- Third, it sets the stage for later publicity.

Watch a local TV news show or examine the local newspaper in any large market, and you are likely to find coverage of a brandstanding event. Corporations have perfected the concept.

Victoria's Secret launched the Wonderbra with brandstanding events. Mars Candy made the Green M&M a cultural icon through brandstanding. The entire fashion industry, as well as professional sports, is based on brandstanding.

The list goes on and on.

With some imagination and a moderate budget, you can brandstand, no matter what the size of your company. Others like you are doing it all the time.

Ever notice, for example, that festivals often get both newspaper and TV coverage. For example, your community may put on an annual Irish festival around St. Patrick's Day. Such events rarely fail to get publicity.

Why?

First, they provide a clear, simple newsworthy theme: "It's St. Patrick's Day and the Irish are celebrating."

Second, they attract large crowds of happy, smiling residents. In this way, they demonstrate to the news media that the event appeals to a targeted audience.

Third, they provide strong visual appeal. You see adults and children dressed in colorful costumes, dancing to lilting music, eating exotic foods and having a good time.

Fourth, they provide a wide window for coverage. The festival goes on for a day or two. There is plenty of time for the TV crew to cover a three-car pile-up and a burning office building, and still shoot footage of the Irish festival.

It's an easy story that viewers like to see. It offers a Targeted Newsworthy Appeal that the news media can comprehend without thinking and can execute with minimum effort.

And that's why it gets covered.

This is the essential appeal of the brandstanding event.

6.2 The Brandstanding Formula

Rather than promote St. Patrick's Day, let's say you want to design your event to promote your business.

The formula for succeeding with a brandstanding event is the same formula that attracts coverage of the local Irish festival. You want to provide:

a. A clear, simple and newsworthy theme.

b. A large crowd of happy, smiling people.

c. Strong visual appeal.

d. A wide window for news coverage.

Let's put this formula to work in an example. Say you run a supermarket and you want publicity that will attract new customers.

6.2a Offer a Clear, Simple and Newsworthy Theme

You could look for an annual observance, preferably one that ties into your customer base. For example, if you do business in a highly ethnic neighborhood, you might choose Cinco de Mayo, or Chinese New Year, or the end of Ramadon. If not, perhaps you would choose something more neutral, like Arbor Day or Veterans Day.

Avoid the obvious holidays like Christmas, Halloween, the Fourth of July or New Year's Day. There's too much competition for the media's attention on those holidays. Whatever holiday you choose, it should suggest strong visuals and good times.

There are other ways to develop a newsworthy theme. You can partner with a charity to sponsor a fund-raising event or a community project. You can do a good deed, like plant trees in a city park or give away backpacks to needy schoolchildren. You can sponsor a participatory stunt, like building the world's largest chocolate sundae.

What ever you choose, it should fit in with your company's central mission. If you make a product, be sure that product is prominently included in the event in some way. If you provide a service, then tie the event to your service.

6.2b Draw a Crowd.

Anything larger than 100 people is plenty, but the more folks the better. If your theme is strong and taps into your customer base, you should have little trouble attracting a crowd.

Look for a common connection, then find a way to celebrate that connection.

Raise money for a charity. Sponsor a festival. Throw a party. Hold a contest. Pull a stunt.

Above all, make it fun.

6.2c Provide Strong Visuals

You need to provide an unusual prop for the photographers to shoot. The more props, the better. The more unusual and colorful, the better.

Whatever your use, either the prop must move or you must have someone interacting with the prop.

If you run a seafood restaurant, display a 100-year-old lobster.

If you own a cheese shop, bring in a two-ton block of cheddar and hire an artist to carve it into a replica of Mount Rushmore.

If you are a dentist, build the world's largest working toothbrush.

Think first, biggest, best.

Think movement and action.

Think big. Dream large.

6.2d Maintain a Wide Window for Media Coverage

Give the local media plenty of opportunity to cover your event. Start in the early morning and keep things going until mid-afternoon. If you can maintain the event for two days, that's even better. Anything longer than two days is pointless for brandstanding.

The optimum times for attracting media coverage are from 10 a.m. to 2 p.m., Monday through Thursday. (Weekends may seem best at first glance. But keep in mind that the news media are like most other businesses. They have fewer workers on hand during weekends. This translates into fewer opportunities to cover your event.)

As an insurance policy, if your budget allows, consider hiring a professional video crew to shoot footage of your event.

Why bother? Because there are many times when TV producers fully intend to cover your event, only to be forced to send all their crews out to cover emergencies like car wrecks and house fires.

If the choice is between your event and an emergency, you will lose every time. Get used to it.

But if you can provide what is known as "B-roll"—professionally filmed footage of your event—you give the producer a way to cover your event without sacrificing coverage of breaking news. It's a win-win.

Don't try to handle B-roll by yourself. This is a time when you will want experienced PR advice. Hire a former TV producer to guide the project. Let the former producer manage the crew, edit the footage, create the news package and deliver the B-roll to every station in your city.

This "insurance policy" will run you about $5,000 to $8,000. But it can salvage your brandstanding event on a busy news day.

6.3 Learn from the Brandstanding Masters

Brandstanding is not for beginners. Never attempt a brandstanding event as your first PR Rainmaking tactic. The best way to learn is to watch your local TV news, take note of brandstanding events that attract broad coverage, and then find out who is behind those events.

Take brandstanders to lunch. Ask questions. Offer to work for free on their next event, just to gain hands-on experience.

The PR Rainmaker knows: When it comes to brandstanding, a little know-how will save you a lot of money.

PR Rainmaking in Action, Part Four:
How to Create News Through Advocacy

7.1 Act Like an Advocate

Advocates use publicity not simply to draw attention to a cause, but also to change behavior.

At their highest level, PR Rainmakers take the same approach. They understand that the best publicity does more than fill a corporate scrapbook; it actually causes its audiences to change their behavior in ways that benefit PR Rainmakers and their companies.

How is this done?

Flacks will tell you that the best method is to "inform the public." In other words, if you present the facts in a logical way, the public will eventually understand your cause, will embrace your solutions and will change its behavior.

Bunk.

Mass psychology simply doesn't work that way. (For that matter, neither does individual psychology.) If it did, then victory in the war for the U.S. videotape industry would have gone to the Beta format, not to VHS.

The human mind is not swayed by facts and logic. Our centers of reason make up only a small percentage of the total human brain. The rest is pure animal.

We delude ourselves into believing our decisions are practical and logical. The truth is that our choices are dominated by impulses, habits and emotions.

We decide based upon illogic, then justify our choices to ourselves with logic.

Thus, the PR Rainmaker knows: When it comes to changing behavior, the catalyst is found in the phrase "enlightened self-interest."

We must stir the public's emotion of self-interest. Then we must use logical enlightenment to help the public justify embracing our solution.

Creating enlightened self-interest comes down to five basic techniques, which may be applied separately, but are most effective when use in concert.

These techniques are:

a. Seize an issue.

b. Enlist third-party leadership.

c. Form activist groups.

d. Provide rationalization.

e. Establish trends.

These are the techniques that mold attitudes and alter behaviors. They are tested by time. PR Rainmakers use all of them to gain advantage.

7.1a Seize an Issue

No successful politician would consider running for any significant office without defining and seizing a key issue.

For Nixon, the issue was law and order. For Reagan, the issue was American pride. For Clinton, the issue was defined by the phrase, "It's the economy, stupid!"

PR Rainmakers look upon their companies (along with products or services) as candidates. They look upon their audiences as voters. They want to win the popular vote for their candidates.

So they look for an issue, define it and make it their own. So can you.

Seek a widespread public problem that your company can solve with its products or its services. Or, look for a public problem that is at least related to your company's mission.

For Glad trash bags, the issue was highway littering. For Ben & Jerry Ice Cream, the issue was corporate responsibility.

So Glad created a national program to clean up litter, sending out more than a million volunteers armed with…what else?…Glad trash bags.

And the Ben & Jerry empire was built upon selling quality ice cream with the promise that a percentage of the profits would be donated to worthy community efforts.

Line your company behind an issue that concerns your audiences. Offer a solution. Take action.

Become an advocate.

7.1b Enlist Third-Party Leadership

The first impulse of the group mind is to follow a leader. Humans look for someone they trust to explain the situation and to give directions.

When the nation is in peril, we turn to the president. When the company is in trouble, we turn to the CEO.

When we want to know how to invest our money, we look to Warren Buffett or Louis Rukyser. When we want to know how to protect ourselves from disease, we turn to Dr. Koop.

When we're looking for a good book to read, we turn to Oprah Winfrey. When we want to learn how to improve our homes, we turn to Martha Stewart or to Bob Vila. When we want to learn how to cook a fabulous meal, we turn to Wolfgang Puck.

When we want to know how to vote, we turn to our political party or to the newspaper's editorial page.

We are in constant search of trusted leaders to advise us on the correct path to take. This is basic human nature.

So it stands to reason that a primary technique in the PR Rainmaker's arsenal is to enlist trusted leaders to champion our cause. The leader brings credibility to our issue and influences the public to change its behavior.

We see examples of this every day in the news, in advertising and through public service announcements.

Gen. Norman Schwarzkopf urges men to consult their doctors about prostate cancer; rock guitarist Frank Zappa tells young adults to become registered voters; NFL quarterback Doug Flutie asks viewers to give money to help autistic children.

So how do PR Rainmakers convince a leader to champion any particular cause? They look for situations where the PR Rainmakers' cause coincides with that of the leader.

Schwarzkopf beat prostate cancer. Zappa battled against Congressional censorship of music. Flutie is the father of an autistic child.

Their interests coincide with those issues. So the leader is generally more than happy to have a forum in which to advance those issues.

7.1c Form Activist Groups

This technique combines the leadership instinct with the herd instinct. Seize an issue, choose a leader and recruit followers. It's an effective formula as old as human history.

It's the basis for political parties from Democrats and Republicans to Communists and Nazis. It's the basis for special interest groups from the American Civil Liberties Union to Greenpeace to the National Organization for Women to the John Birch Society. It's the basis for civic organizations from the Rotary Club to the Red Cross.

Groups inspire action. They take on problems, advance causes and offer solutions. They educate and they intimidate. And they get more news coverage than do most individuals.

All of this makes the group a highly effective method for changing mass behavior.

7.1d Provide Rationalization

While facts and logic alone will never convince the mass mind to act in your favor, a steady stream of reason will support the decisions that the crowd makes at the emotional level.

That's the way the mind works. We make decisions with our emotions, then support those decisions with the facts that we choose to believe.

The PR Rainmaker knows: Most people rationalize rather than reason.

Prompting that rationalization is the job of Web sites, brochures, pamphlets, posters, white papers, guest columns, public service announcements, opinion pieces, studies, surveys and all of the other informational documents that are generated by most PR campaigns.

These pieces become even more effective when authored, fronted or supported by a third-party champion.

Example: Why was the "safe sex" condom campaign of the 1980s effective? Because it found a champion in the surgeon general, Dr. C. Everett Koop. Think how much less effective the campaign would have been if fronted by America's condom manufacturers.

Why, in the 1990s, did Archer Daniels Midland hire journalist David Brinkley to talk about the need to alleviate world hunger through just the advanced agricultural techniques that ADM uses to generate its revenues? Would the company's CEO been less effective? Yes. Why? Because he would lack the third party status of a Brinkley.

The lesson is clear.

Yes, you want to provide a steady stream of interpretive information. But whenever possible, attribute that information to a credible third party.

7.1e Establish Trends

Another trait of human nature is the need to follow the crowd. To jump on the bandwagon. To fit in.

Few humans are willing to stand apart from others. This is why are anxious to wear the proper attire to any given social function. This is why most of us live in three-bedroom, two-bath homes. This is why we allow peer pressure to cause us to buy things we don't really want and to do things we don't really want to do.

This is the instinct that leads to fashion and to fad. It's what causes most of us to watch certain TV shows, see certain movies and listen to certain pop songs.

We see a trend and we join the herd. We can't help ourselves. This is a survival instinct that is deeply ingrained by our evolutionary history.

PR Rainmakers recognize the need for trends in human society. They put this instinct to work.

Want to sell more pianos? Then encourage architects to include music rooms in their home designs.

Want to sell aphrodisiacs? Then publish a study that shows more American couples are engaging in sexual activity well into their senior years.

Want to sell more polo shirts and khakis? Then encourage office managers to observe "Casual Fridays" to improve employee morale.

Most Americans want to identify and to understand the trends that are all around them. This explains our obsession with surveys, polls and studies. We want to know what to do and want permission to do it.

PR Rainmakers grant that permission by launching, identifying, defining and demonstrating a clear trend.

7.2 How Advocacy Creates News

Each step along the road to advocacy is an opportunity to create news.

Your company defines an issue and vows to solve it. That's news.

A third-party leader agrees to champion your cause. That's news.

A group is formed to help your company solve the problem. That's news.

The byproducts of rationalization—studies, surveys, white papers, opinion pieces, speeches—are all opportunities to create news.

A trend that is clear and profound is always good fodder for news.

And at each stop, your company increases its credibility while raising its profile.

The community looks upon your company in a new light. You are seen as a leader as well as an expert.

Customers and clients turn to you for solutions before they consider your competition.

This is PR Rainmaking at its most effective.

This is your goal.

PR Rainmaking in Action, Part Five: How to Give Your Story the 'People' Treatment

8.1 Why Young is Better Than Old

OK, suppose you don't have time to conduct a survey or to become an advocate. Suppose you don't have the inclination to build a Trojan Horse or to stage a brandstanding event.

Suppose all you really want is a sure-fire method for attracting media attention to your company, your product, your cause.

Then you want to master the "*People*" Treatment.

The term refers to *People* magazine, the grocery check-out publication that is read each week by an estimated 32.4 million Americans. Perhaps no other outlet in the last 25 years has so successfully tapped into the psyche of the typical media consumer.

People magazine has accomplished this by adhering to a well-conceived formula for choosing the subjects of its stories and its covers. Here are the rules:

1. Young is better than old.

2. Pretty is better than ugly.

3. Rich is better than poor.

4. TV is better than music.

5. Music is better than movies.

6. Movies are better than sports.

7. Anything is better than politics.

8. And nothing is better than the celebrity dead.

8.2 The Face Makes All the Difference

The formula is the result of measurable statistics. The magazine has found—through trial and error—that displaying certain celebrity archetypes on *People's* cover will tend to either boost or depress its single-copy sales.

For example, the editors discovered early that putting billionaire J. Paul Getty, or sports commentator Howard Cosell, or vice presidential candidate Tom Eagleton on the cover was certain to lead to low sales.

However, the magazine found it could boost its sales by putting attractive newsmakers out front: Prince William, Madonna, Brooke Shields, Jennifer Lopez, Ben Affleck, John Travolta, Britney Spears, Charlie Sheen, Cher, Katie Couric, Michael Jackson, Jane Fonda, Farrah Fawcett, Elizabeth Taylor, Winona Ryder, and on and on.

For sales to soar, the editors found, what People really needed was the tragic death of a celebrity. The death of Princess Diana sold 2.99 million copies, the death of rock musician John Lennon sold 2.64 million and the death of Princess Grace sold 2.62 million.

The *People* Treatment extends to its inside stories. And savvy companies have learned to exploit this:

- Toyota gained People coverage for its revolutionary Prius, which uses an electric motor and a gasoline engine to cut emissions by 75 percent while getting 52 miles to the gallon. How? By asking a Prius owner to pose while filling up his car with gas. The owner is movie star Leonardo DiCaprio.

- A carnival to benefit the Glaser Pediatric AIDS Foundation got a two-page spread of photos in People. How? By bringing in celebrities like movie star Tom Cruise and skateboard champ Tony Hawk.

- Physician Harvey Karp landed a two-page story in People touting his method of calming crying infants as well as his new book, "The Happiest Baby on the Block." How? By pointing out that his clients include actors Michelle Pfeiffer and Pierce Brosnan.

This is the essence of the *People* Treatment: Find some way to tie a celebrity to your story.

What do Leo DiCaprio, Tony Hawk, Tom Cruise, Michelle Pfeiffer and Pierce Brosnan have in common? They are attractive and successful. They all fit the *People* formula.

8.3 Celebrity and Human Instinct

So why does the *People* formula work so well? What is behind our fascination with celebrities?

One media psychologist believes that celebrity taps deeply into a common need that is rooted in our evolutionary past.

"If you go back to the primates," psychologist Stuart Fischoff told the Los Angeles Times, "you see that there were always alpha males who all the rest of us had to groom and flatter and give all our attention to. If we didn't pay attention to these early 'celebrities,' we wouldn't get food and we wouldn't get attention."

Today, modern humans are saddled with an "elaboration of that early survival system," Fischoff says.

"Though the celebrities are no longer responsible for keeping us safe or well-fed," he says, "we still seem to be programmed to need them in our lives."

8.4 Feeding the Media's Hunger for Celebrity

We have become a nation obsessed with celebrity, and the media know that the surest way to get the attention of a reader or a viewer is to include a celebrity.

In today's media jungle, there's too much at stake for any journalist to ignore the draw of celebrity.

"People is a must-read for me," CBS anchor Dan Rather told the *Washington Post*. "I am a hard-news guy, but I'm also a hard-news guy trying to last…A lot of our viewers read People and I should be reading at least some of what they read."

PBS news commentator Daniel Schorr agrees. "The bottom line," he told the *Post*, "on celebrity journalism is that it does sell."

The truth is that the *People* formula will work with virtually any outlet in any medium. It works as well for getting into *USA Today* or *CNN Headline News* as it does for attracting coverage from small-town newspapers and trade magazines.

The lesson for the PR Rainmaker: The surest route to positive media coverage is to carefully tie a celebrity to your story.

"Carefully" means to use the same judgment that the editors of People use in choosing their cover celebrities. Each week's choice can swing *People's* newsstand sales by a million copies. You should make your choice of celebrities as if you have just as much at stake.

Choose the young over the old, the beautiful over the ugly and the rich over the poor.

Yes, this is shallow. But in today's media environment, shallow works.

Judy Kessler, a former *People* reporter, expressed this philosophy best in her 1994 book, *Inside People*, when she wrote:

"Readers are in a hurry. We want to amuse them, but not confuse them."

The PR Rainmaker keeps this in mind at all times, particularly when applying the *People* Treatment.

8.5 Putting the *People* Treatment to Work

There is far more to the *People* Treatment than simply hiring a celebrity to attend a grand opening. It's a technique that can be applied again and again by any enterprise that is willing to combine creativity with audacity.

There are two ways to bring a celebrity into your story: directly and indirectly.

The first is the direct approach, which makes a clear connection between your company and a celebrity. The best way is to attract a celebrity as a customer or a participant.

If you run a public company, consider adding a celebrity to your board of directors. If you run a private company, consider bringing in a celebrity as a high-profile partner.

If you are staging an event, invite—or even hire—a celebrity to take an active role. The key word is "active." Just showing up won't cut it. The celebrity must commit an overt act that will give the media some news to report. This act can be as simple as reading to children, passing out pamphlets or even cutting a ribbon. But news requires action, so the celebrity must act.

The indirect approach requires more creativity and more audacity. To make it work, you must find a way to "piggy-back" on celebrities and the news they generate.

Does your medical practice offer the same treatment that allowed an overweight movie star to lose 150 pounds? Can your investment company suggest a list of tactics that would have helped keep a famous rock musician from filing bankruptcy? Does your company manufacture a device that could have kept a famous designer from drowning in her swimming pool?

If so, tell the news media. The odds are very good that you will attract attention.

It doesn't matter that it wasn't you who treated the overweight star, who consulted the bankrupt musician or who installed the designer's pool. What matters is that you offer something very similar to what these celebrities want or need, and that you are able to tie your offering into the news these celebrities generate.

To make the indirect approach work, you must move quickly. Keep an eye on the Internet news pages, particularly any devoted to entertainment, sports and other celebrity-based news.

Look for opportunities where what you offer is very close to what a celebrity wants or needs. Then strike immediately.

Work the journalists with whom you have developed a relationship. Shoot them an e-mail that briefly explains the connection between your offering and the celebrity who is making news. A fax or a phone call will work as well.

In any case, make a one-to-one contact with your targeted journalists just as swiftly as you can. You can't be shy when applying the *People* Treatment.

You must piggy-back on today's news. Tomorrow is too late.

In Conclusion:
The PR Rainmaker vs.
the Five Biggest Mistakes in PR

9.1 PR's Five Biggest Mistakes and How to Avoid Them

Flacks make the same mistakes over and over. They've made them for so long, they no longer recognize them as mistakes. And yet day after day, year after year, these mistakes sap away their client's PR budget with little in return.

The PR Rainmaker recognizes these mistakes for what they are: vampires that feed upon our time, energy and resources.

9.2a Mistake No. 1: Thinking Tactics Over Strategy

Most PR specialists are tremendous at executing tactics. They can put together beautiful media kits. They can whip up a wonderful media list. They can cobble together a press release within hours.

What most PR specialists lack is the ability to use these tactics in concert. In other words, they can't devise a strategy for using their tactics in an coordinated, effective way.

Indeed, most PR specialists fail to see a difference between a strategy and a tactic.

As a result, they fail to impress those who think strategically: their CEO, their company's legal counsel or their company's marketing director.

In contrast, PR Rainmakers are serious students of strategy. They read Sun Tzu, Machiavelli and Clausewitz. They study political/military history, and apply its lessons to the situations they face daily.

They develop a strategy, then choose the appropriate tactics.

9.2b Mistake No. 2: Emphasizing Frequency Over Impact

Most PR specialists like to count clips as their primary measure of success. That's how they keep score.

They forget that the primary purpose of all public relations is to influence the public through credibility.

What does it matter how many newspapers, TV stations, radio stations and Web sites notice your message if that message fails to sway the public?

The PR Rainmaker knows that one "hit" that moves the public in the right direction is worth a million hits that fail.

9.2c Mistake No. 3: Measuring Equivalence Rather Than Influence

Somewhere along the way in PR's circuitous history, some genius decided to use "advertising equivalence" as the standard for measuring a campaign's success.

This is done by measuring the column inches or the broadcast time that covers a campaign's message, then multiplying by the medium's advertising rate.

For example, if the campaign scored a 20-inch news story, and the newspaper charges $100 per column inch, then the story is worth an advertising equivalence of $2,000. Most PR firms take this a step further, claiming that a news story is four times more effective than advertising, thus the story is worth $8,000.

This measure is used to justify the PR fee. If the PR agency charges the client $1,000 to produce the clip, and the clip is worth $8,000 in advertising equivalence, then that's a bargain, right?

Clients seem to be comfortable with this approach. But advertising equivalence is a disservice to both the interests of the client and to the value of public relations.

The only measure of a PR campaign should be the influence it has over the public mind. And the only way to measure influence is with opinion polling.

The process is simple.

First, you scientifically survey your target audiences to learn what they think about your issue, what messages are likely to sway them to your side, and which leaders are most likely to deliver that message effectively.

Second, you design and launch a campaign based upon your research.

Third, you survey again to find out if your campaign has changed your targets' thinking.

If your audiences now agree with your message and are changing their behaviors accordingly, your campaign is a success. If they still disagree, your campaign is a failure.

There is no other valid measure for PR, and the PR Rainmaker knows it.

9.2d Mistake No. 4: Preferring Cheap Over Effective

In a misguided effort to market against advertising agencies, PR agencies will often preach that public relations is less expensive than advertising.

This is true. But the impression many clients get is that PR is cheap. That is false.

An effective PR campaign is an expensive undertaking. Not as expensive as advertising, but expensive nonetheless. Even if you do the PR yourself, as will many entrepreneurs and professionals, you will expend a great deal of time instead of money.

The result of Mistake No. 4 is to either mislead the client into expecting a small bill, or to force the PR specialist to work with a budget that will not support the campaign.

This cheats everyone involved and has led to much of the current dissatisfaction with PR among top corporate executives.

9.2e Mistake No. 5: Letting the Boss Run the Campaign

Most folks who choose PR as a career are nice people.

Very, very, very nice.

Too damn nice.

The reason? Most PR specialists put a higher value on being liked than upon being respected.

As a result, they tend to let others overrule their judgment. They all too readily give in to the Boss.

The Boss may be the company's CEO. It may be the marketing director. It may be the legal counsel.

In any case, the Boss rarely knows anything about dealing with the news media or about influencing public opinion. Yet the Boss often suffers from the delusion that both are easily managed and manipulated.

Need good press? Fire off a news release. How hard can that be, right?

Well, here's a bit of news for all the Bosses out there who believe they understand the news media and public opinion: You may know how to read a newspaper. You may know how to turn on a TV. You may even know how to surf the Internet. But none of that qualifies you to serve as your own PR counsel.

Of course, the PR "profession" has no one to blame but itself for this attitude among our Bosses. We have failed to establish ourselves as true professionals, along the order of lawyers and doctors. We have no firm methods or processes. We have no enforceable credentials. We have no governing body with the power to enforce professional standards.

Instead, we merely take on the trappings of a profession, much as have our counterparts in journalism.

The fact is, anyone can claim to be a public relations counsel. Until that changes, how can we expect to receive respect from the Boss?

9.3 The PR Rainmaker's Solutions

So how do PR Rainmakers avoid these mistakes?

First, we study strategy and learn to apply it to the tactics we already know so well.

Second, we stop counting clips and start measuring the actual effective influence of our campaigns.

Third, we refuse to compare PR to advertising and insist upon distinguishing our work as valuable and crucial in its own unique way.

Fourth, we stop talking about PR as a cheap alternative to advertising, and we start talking about how effective PR can be when executed in a proper, intelligent and well-financed manner.

Fifth, we increase our own credibility and effectiveness by earning MBAs, law degrees and other well-recognized signs of advanced education. We seek and we hire those prospects who have earned these degrees, and we pay them well.

Above all, we push hard for PR to become a true profession.

For now, we must console ourselves by recognizing that, as a recognized field of study, public relations is just a century old. It took both medicine and law far longer than 100 years to discipline themselves into true professions.

The good news is: The tide of history is on the side of the PR Rainmaker.

About the Author

Rusty Cawley spent more than two decades in the news media as a reporter, editor and publisher. Today, he serves as the director of media relations for one of the largest independent public relations agencies in Dallas.

Cawley advises a wide range of clients on the proper and successful use of PR Rainmaking techniques. He also teaches these techniques to executives, professionals and entrepreneurs through his speeches, seminars, workshops and his Web site, **www.PRrainmaker.com**.

0-595-24399-1